The establishment of the Christian Church throughout the world is due in large measure to its heroic local pioneers. But all too often we have overlooked these dedicated leaders, preferring, instead, to cast the spotlight on our missionaries.

In this book Dr. John T. Seamands seeks to rectify this situation and to give due credit and praise to these national Christians —these men and women who sacrificed and toiled, suffered and died, that their own people might come to be Christians. The list is long; the fifteen described here are merely representative.

They are indeed an interesting and variegated group. They come from high caste and low caste, from rich parents and poor parents; from Christian homes and from non-Christian ones; from noble families and primitive tribes. Some were educated; others untutored, knowing only how to read and write. But all had one thing in common— they could not keep quiet about their faith and led their people to the Christian life.

Pioneers
of
the
Younger
Churches

Pioneers

of

the

Younger

Churches

JOHN T. SEAMANDS

NASHVILLE
ABINGDON PRESS
NEW YORK

PIONEERS OF THE YOUNGER CHURCHES

Copyright © 1967 by Abingdon Press

Library of Congress Catalog Card Number: 67-22166

SET UP, PRINTED, AND BOUND BY THE
PARTHENON PRESS, AT NASHVILLE,
TENNESSEE, UNITED STATES OF AMERICA

Dedicated

to

my

Indian

Colleagues

in loving appreciation
of their sacrificial and faithful work
in building the Church of Jesus Christ in India

Preface

DURING THE PAST four hundred years and more, the churches of the West have been proclaiming the Good News of Jesus Christ to the peoples of the East. They have been sending their representatives and sharing their resources.

As a result, today the Christian Church has been planted in almost every land around the world. It can be found in the foothills of the Himalaya Mountains and on the plains of the Indus basin. It can be found in the sprawling metropolises of Japan and in the remote villages of Africa. It can be found on the vast archipelago of Indonesia and on the scattered islands of the Pacific. Its fellowship includes Bataks from Sumatra, Karens from Burma, Ibans from Sarawak, Chinese businessmen from Singapore, students from Japan, farmers from Korea, soldiers from Formosa, outcastes from India, and bushmen from Africa. Its membership includes those who were formerly Hindu, Buddhist, Muslim, Confucianist, Shintoist, and animist. This is the miracle of the modern period of Christian missions.

7

In the establishment of these so-called Younger Churches, foreign missionaries played a leading role. They were a courageous band, ready to face any danger and make any sacrifice for the salvation and uplift of their fellowmen. Commissioned by God and constrained by Christ's love, they crossed the seas and climbed the mountains, entering every continent and setting foot on every island. They mastered difficult languages, adjusted to alien cultures, and made themselves at home in strange surroundings. They preached, taught, healed, and suffered. Many were struck down in their early youth by strange diseases; several were martyred by hostile men. We bow in humble respect before this long line of splendor.

But in remembering the missionaries we dare not forget the host of native men and women who played a significant role in the building of their Churches. They also sacrificed and toiled, suffered and died in the service of their Master. Knowing the language and customs, and understanding the mind and heart of their own people, they were able to penetrate into the life of their nation to a far greater degree than the foreign missionary. Some who came into the Christian Church out of alien religious backgrounds not only had the distinct advantage of knowing and understanding the heart of these faiths; but they were able to communicate the Christian message to their adherents in a much more meaningful way than the foreign missionary.

This book is an attempt to give honor to this magnificent host of native Christian leaders, who came out of every tribe and nation. It is by no means exhaustive, for the list of heroes is far too long. It is merely representative, with a few of the most illustrious names in the history of the Younger Churches.

The Church builders whose biographies appear in this book are indeed an interesting and variegated group. They came from dissimilar backgrounds and from different levels of society—from high caste and low caste, from rich parents and poor parents, from Christian homes and pagan homes, from noble clans and primitive tribes. Some were educated, with high degrees; others were untutored, knowing only how to read and write. Some were prominent leaders; others were obscure helpers. But all had one important fact in common —they were transformed by the same wonderful Savior and were fully dedicated to his will.

These servants of God were endowed with a variety of gifts and performed diverse services in the life of the Church. All were pioneers, some were administrators; some were evangelists, others missionaries; some were educators, others reformers. They all worked together for the development and witness of the Church of Jesus Christ.

One fact is thus made clear. God uses all types of people in the building of his Church. There is a place and a task for each one.

JOHN T. SEAMANDS
Willmore, Kentucky

Contents

I

Trailblazers

*"I have laid the foundation, and
another buildeth thereon."* I CORINTHIANS 3:10

MANY OF THE Younger Churches are the result of vigorous group movements in which large numbers of families and even whole villages have come into the Church in rapid succession. Such movements were invariably born out of, and carried forward by, the sustained witness of devoted laymen and laywomen, who in their own simple way shared the love of Christ with their relatives, neighbors, and friends.

Ko Tha Byu of Burma, and Chi-oang and Do-wai of Taiwan are outstanding examples of the innumerable host of faithful and effective witnesses who just could not keep silent about their faith. Though separated by a continent in distance and almost a century in time, they had several things in common. They came from tribal areas, from a background of animism. They were simple people with little education, but their ministry was intense. Constrained by the love of Christ, they had one magnificent obsession—to lead their people to the feet of the Master by whose grace their own lives had been so marvelously transformed. The two Younger Churches that they helped to establish are today living memorials of their devotion and witness.

1

Ko Tha Byu
of Burma

THE STORY OF the introduction of Christianity among
Burma's primitive Karen people is one of the most wonderful in Christian missions. Out of this oppressed race Christ
has created a new people. Anyone who goes today among
Christian Karen villages, sees tidy homes and dress, little
schoolhouses built and maintained by their own contributions, and hears church bells summon them to listen to the
preaching of the gospel by their own pastors. One can hardly
believe that a century or more ago their ancestors were a
most undeveloped people, without property, education, or
hope. Karens today are living witnesses of the gospel's transforming power.

When Baptist missionaries first arrived in Burma, the
Karens were a subject people found throughout the country
but located for the most part in jungle areas. Numbering
about one-tenth of the population, these people were cul-
turally and linguistically different from the Burmese, by
whom they had been despised and oppressed for so long

that they had become a timid, irresolute, and servile people, given to offensive habits and strong drink. They were called "wild men of the jungle" or "Karen pigs" by the Burmese and treated with disdain. A common saying among the Burmese was, "You can teach a buffalo, but you can't teach a Karen."

And yet the Karens, though illiterate, were far from being an inferior people. Religiously, they were in some ways superior to their more educated and cultured Buddhist Burmese neighbors. Animists by religion, they had traditions which seem to have served as a real preparation for the Christian message. They knew of the Creator God, were strongly opposed to idolatry, and had a high regard for marital fidelity. They had a story of the fall through which they had lost the favor of God and been reduced to their quasi-servile position. They believed also that in times past they once possessed a sacred book, which their fathers had lost through carelessness. When a preacher came, bearing a sacred book and telling them that the God whose anger they had incurred had himself come to seek them in mercy in Jesus Christ, it seemed to them that their dreams and hopes had all been realized. Whereas Burmese were slow to accept the Good News, Karens accepted it with readiness and came into the Christian Church by hundreds and thousands.

The human agent in evangelizing these people illustrates afresh how God uses the most unlikely men. He was a robber and a murderer, a slave of violent temper, indolent and ignorant. Yet he became a faithful and effective evangelist, a distinguished instrument in the hands of God to arouse the attention of the Karen race to the Christian faith.

Ko Tha Byu was born about the year 1778 at a village called U Twa, which at that time was a four days' journey north of Bassein. He was a wayward and ungovernable lad with an unusually violent temper. At the age of fifteen he ran away from home, joined himself to evil companions, and in the course of time became a robber and a murderer. How many of his fellow countrymen he murdered, either as principal or accomplice, it is difficult to say; but it was at least thirty according to his own confession.

After the war between England and Burma, Ko Tha Byu, in his late forties, went to Rangoon and found employment in the household of the Reverend Mr. Hough, a pioneer Baptist missionary to Burma. There he received his first religious impressions, and to the end of his life he always remembered "Teacher Hough" with great affection, often making mention of him in his public prayers.

Leaving the employ of Hough, he fell into trouble and was put up for sale as a slave in the Moulmein Bazaar on account of his debts. (According to Burmese law at that time, a debtor became a slave to his creditor.) Fortunately, Ko Shwe Be, a Burmese Christian and disciple of Adoniram Judson, came across Ko Tha Byu, paid twelve Rupees for him (about $4.50), and took him into his household as a servant. He tried his best to instruct him in the Christian faith but made little progress. Tha Byu's fiery temper and evil habits proved too much for his master's patience, so finally Ko Shwe Be handed him over to Adoniram Judson, who agreed to assume the responsibility for Tha Byu's debts.

Slowly Judson began to make an impression on this hardened criminal. Tha Byu began to take an increasing interest in the Christian faith and even learned to read, somewhat falteringly, the Burmese New Testament. It was not very long before he began to show signs of repentance. His past life, however, made it extremely difficult for him to believe that God would receive and forgive so vile a sinner. In addition, his violent temper often depressed him and discouraged him from praying. At last his faith gained in strength, and he openly confessed Christ as his personal

Savior. With great joy the missionaries perceived a marked improvement in his character. The little Burmese congregation, however, was very slow to accept him into their fellowship, for he had not gained complete victory over his passionate temper, and they could not believe that he had been truly "born again." But after a year there was such a transformation in the life of Ko Tha Byu that the church was convinced of his conversion, agreed to accept him for membership, and appointed a date for his public baptism.

Meanwhile another Karen family, along with a young woman and her two small brothers, orphans and relatives of the family, made their appearance in Moulmein. As they were in a most miserable condition, without food and shelter, the Baptist missionaries gave the family a place in which to live, took the young woman into the girls' school, and placed the two boys in Mr. George Boardman's school for boys. The young woman, Naw Ma E, made good progress in the school. After a few months she became the wife of Ko Tha Byu.

Shortly before the day of Ko Byu's baptism arrived, the Reverend and Mrs. Boardman set sail from Moulmein down the coast of Southern Burma, to begin work in a new mission station at Tavoy. They wanted to take the two little Karen boys with them, and Ko Tha Byu decided to accompany them, as his wife was unwilling to be separated from her brothers. His baptism was accordingly deferred until after their arrival in Tavoy. On May 16, 1828, Mr. Boardman performed the happy ceremony, and Ko Tha Byu, at the age of fifty, became the first convert of the Karen people. This event is recorded by Mr. Boardman in his journal:

Repaired early this morning to a neighboring tank and administered baptism to Ko Tha Byu, the Karen Christian who accompanied us from Moulmein. May we often have the joy of witnessing such scenes. The three Karen visitors were present. They appear to be impressed with the truth of our doctrine. They have urged Ko Tha Byu to accompany them and I have left it for him to decide. He concluded to go. Perhaps God has a work for him to do among his countrymen. He is very zealous in declaring what he knows.[1]

The following year, in the month of March, Naw Ma E followed the example of her husband and became the first woman convert among the Karens.

Immediately after his baptism, Ko Tha Byu left Tavoy to visit Karen settlements in the surrounding villages. In his simple yet sincere way, he taught his people the rudiments of Christian faith and witnessed to the transforming power of Christ in his own life. In one little settlement on Khat creek he was received with much courtesy and interest, and upon his return to the city two of the men accompanied him to the missionary's home. After further instruction they were baptized by Mr. Boardman, thus becoming the first fruits of Ko Tha Byu's labors. One of the men, Maung Khway, was brother to the chief of the village. After a second visit to the settlement, Ko Tha Byu returned with ten new converts, one of them Maung So, the chief himself.

Not long afterward the mother of Maung So died, and, fearing that their relatives might wish to perform the customary pagan funeral rites, Maung So erected a preaching *zayat* (a crudely built assembly hall) near the grave and invited Ko Tha Byu to join him in preaching "the Word of Life," while the others were engaged in their ceremonies. As a result of this preaching mission, several became interested

---

[1] Dr. Francis Mason, *The Memoir of Ko Tha Byu*, p. 8. Quoted by permission of The Burma Baptist Convention Board of Publications, Rangoon, Burma.

in the Christian faith, and twelve inquirers returned to Tavoy with Ko Tha Byu to learn more about The Way. Two of the men were headmen of villages. In the course of time, the entire inhabitants of Maung So's village were won to Christ.

Visits to other Karen settlements met with similar success. The village people listened to Ko Tha Byu's witness and preaching with great enthusiasm, and each time he returned to the mission center he brought a group of inquirers with him. From one of these early tours he brought back about forty candidates for instruction and baptism. An entry in Mr. Boardman's journal at this time says: "A good number of Karens are now with us, and Ko Tha Byu is engaged day and night in reading and explaining to them the words of eternal life. It seems as though the time for favoring this people has come." [2]

At times Mr. Boardman accompanied the Karen evangelist on his visits to surrounding villages. After Mr. Boardman preached in Burmese, Ko Tha Byu would interpret as much of the discourse as he could remember into the Karen language. In this way, whether at home or out on tour, the two men worked in close cooperation, supplementing each other's labors with their own particular gifts.

While at home between tours, Ko Tha Byu was busily engaged in searching out Karens who visited the city on business. On one occasion he found a young Karen who had embraced the Buddhist religion, fasting in the niche of a pagoda in the hope of obtaining a great reward in the next life. Ko Tha Byu talked to him about Christ and invited him to come to the missionary's home for instruction in the Christian faith. After a few days with Mr. Boardman, the inquirer took a Christian book with him and returned to his

[2] *Ibid.,* p. 12.

village. In a few days he was back with three of his relatives, all anxious to know more about the way of salvation.

On another occasion Ko Tha Byu contacted a very respectable-looking old Karen, who was the chief of his race in the province of Mergui. After listening to the evangelist's testimony, the chief implored Ko Tha Byu to accompany him to Mergui, promising him that he would be escorted from one Karen settlement to another until he reached his own province again. Taking along a Christian companion, Ko Tha Byu headed south on an expedition which he realized would be fraught with many difficulties, but at the same time promised great opportunities. Unfortunately, he became ill during the early part of the trip and was never able to reach Mergui. More interested in the salvation of others than in his own comfort, however, he insisted that his companion continue the preaching tour alone, while he remained behind to recuperate at a town called Palouk. As soon as he was well enough to travel again, he reluctantly headed back toward Tavoy, traveling slowly and preaching in all the Karen settlements along the way. It is interesting to note that the man with whom Ko Tha Byu stayed in Palouk was the first person to be baptized in that settlement a few years later and became one of the pillars of the church. Also, in 1837, the chief himself became a Christian and was baptized by the Reverend Mr. Mason, successor to Mr. Boardman. Many of his relatives and subjects followed his example.

Meanwhile, Mr. Boardman's health failed considerably, making it impossible for him to carry on his ministry of evangelism and teaching. With the very important exception of Mrs. Boardman's invaluable labors with people who visited Tavoy, for the next two years the whole care of the church and teaching of inquirers became the responsibility of Ko Tha Byu. The good number of baptisms during this period

afford the best comment upon his labors. During the rainy
season each year, he conducted a primary school in one
of the Christian settlements. His diligence in this phase of
the work was as conspicuous as in every other in which he
engaged. Some of his students at the close of school could
repeat verbatim several Burmese tracts.

When the Reverend Mr. Mason arrived at Tavoy, Ko Tha
Byu was released from his manifold duties and set free once
again for the work of evangelism, which was the joy of
his life. Early in the year 1833, he left Tavoy, and after
spending a month or two preaching in and around Moulmein,
he proceeded on to the capital city, Rangoon. At that time
the Karens of the Irrawaddy Delta had never heard the
gospel, as no teachers either native or foreign had ever
visited them. They did not know that their language had
been reduced to writing and a tract printed in it; neither
had they heard that any of their countrymen had embraced
the Christian faith.

The next few months were a period of intense activity for
Ko Tha Byu. With a Burmese Christian for a guide, he
traveled and preached incessantly in the Karen villages in
the vicinity of Rangoon. Wading through waters up to
his chest and often meeting with opposition from Buddhists,
in village after village he distributed tracts, visited homes,
prayed with inquirers, and preached in bazaars. His sincere
labors and earnest appeals were not in vain. Very soon
fruit began to appear, and inquirers multiplied.

By October of that same year, in desperation the Reverend
Mr. Bennet, one of the Baptist missionaries in Rangoon,
wrote to his superintendent, Dr. Adoniram Judson:

We are in distress and send to you for relief. For the last
several days, our house and the house of Ko Tha Byu, ten cubits
square, have been thronged. . . . Karens are thronging us from

Dalla, Leing, Hmawbi, Kyadan, and many places I have never heard named; men, women, and children are all anxiously inquiring about the religion of Jesus. They are all eager for schools, and offer to build *zayats* for preaching if some one will come to teach them. There are very many who already keep our Sunday, read our tracts, and try to teach one another as best they can. They read these tracts daily and all get together in families and sing and pray to our God. The heads of the families not only do this, but they teach their children. They declare that they have left off drinking spirit, and, as far as they understand, try to practice the teachings of our Scriptures.

What shall we do? Ko Tha Byu is only one among a thousand. He cannot preach the Gospel and teach these people to read in their own language at the same time. We want one man to go to Bassein; another to go up to Prome, and along the river; another to Hmawbi and vicinity, towards old Pegu—all these to preach the Gospel; and we certainly need as many more for school masters. Can you send us any assistance? If so, do; for Christ and His cause require it. Oh! could we go among these people as freely and easily as in the provinces, I have no doubt hundreds would be added to the Lord.

P.S. Ko Tha Byu complains that the Karens throng his house so that it is breaking down.[3]

As small congregations began to form around Rangoon in several of the villages, some of the leading Karen laymen from the Moulmein area came over to help in conducting regular worship services and household prayers. They also taught a good number of the newly baptized Christians how to read and write. The only printed resources they had at the time were a solitary tract and a spelling book.

Persecution broke out in the town of Hmawbi where Ko Tha Byu was making his headquarters, so he was forced to flee northward to Pegu, an important city on the river. This turned out to be in favor of the gospel, for about two thou-

[3] *Ibid.,* pp. 20-21.

sand Karens lived in the vicinity. It wasn't long before many
of them heard the good news of Christ from the tireless
evangelist and asked for public baptism. In this way "a great
and effectual door" was opened to the central part of Burma.

By the latter part of 1837, Ko Tha Byu's health began
to fail. He was now about fifty-nine years of age, afflicted
with rheumatism and partial blindness. His days of strenuous
itineration were over. He returned to Moulmein, the place
of his conversion, and for the next two years or more, as
his physical condition permitted, he ministered to the Christians, nurturing and encouraging them in the faith.

In February, 1840, the Reverend Mr. Abbott, a Baptist
missionary in Moulmein, was appointed to a new evangelistic
mission in Arakan province, along the coast of the Bay of
Bengal. In spite of his weakness, Ko Tha Byu requested Mr.
Abbott for permission to accompany him to Sandoway, with
his family, so that he might witness to his fellow Karens living
in that section. Upon their arrival, Mr. Abbott sent him to
a small Karen village, where he remained all the time he
spent in Arakan, witnessing to inquirers who came to his
home. Within a few months, the first four converts had been
baptized and several others were awaiting the ordinance.

But here in the midst of his labors, the summons came
for Ko Tha Byu to cease from his work. By early September
his rheumatic complaint had become so distressing that he
was unable to rise from his bed. Soon the disease settled in
his lungs, causing violent inflammation and excessive pain.
Suffering made him very irritable at times and his old
temper would occasionally show itself, but on the whole he
bore the pain bravely and calmly, until death brought rest
to his feeble body, on the ninth of September, 1840. He was
buried in a simple grave in the hills of Arakan, just outside
the village where four had been led to Christ as a result of
his witness. No mound marks his grave; no storied urn or

animated bust indicates his last resting place; but the eternal
mountains are his monument, and Christian villages that
today clothe their sides are his epitaph.

Ko Tha Byu was a humble and faithful servant of his
Master. In intellectual ability he was greatly limited. His
slow mind could never apprehend the full message of the
gospel. He was never ordained by the mission for "he simply
was not adapted for the pastoral office." But he was an
unceasing and tireless pioneer, seeking out places where the
foreign missionary could not go. He was constantly endeavor-
ing to enlarge his area of activity, pushing out from Tavoy
to the border of Siam—where he was turned back by officials
—and then northward to Moulmein, Rangoon, Pegu, Bassein,
and Sandoway. His task was to open up doors for the
missionaries, to make initial contacts, and to arouse the
interest of people. He led inquirers as far as he could, then
left missionaries to take them from there. A contemporary
mission worker said of him, "Ko Tha Byu was an ignorant
man; and yet he did more good than all of us, for God was
with him."

Ko Tha Byu had a passion for preaching; it was his
ruling passion. On one occasion while he was out in a boat
with one of the missionaries at Moulmein, he was in
evident danger of losing his life. He cried out, not for God
to have mercy on his soul as might have been expected, but
"Alas, I shall be drowned and never more preach the Word
of God to the Karens!"

In every other work he was indolent and inefficient; while
in preaching Christ crucified, his soul would be wrought up
with more than human energy. He was always planning some
new excursion and never was so happy as when he found
individuals to whom he might preach from morning until
evening. In seasons of special interest he not only continued

in speech, like Paul, until midnight but not infrequently till break of day.

As to the abiding fruit of Ko Tha Byu's labors, on visiting one settlement which had been evangelized by him, one of the missionaries wrote:

I cry no longer, "the horrors of heathenism," but "the blessings of missions" . . . . Heathenism has fled these banks. . . . I am seated in the midst of a Christian village, surrounded by a people that love as Christians, converse as Christians, act like Christians, and look like Christians. If it be worth a voyage across the Atlantic to see the Shenandoah run through the Blue Ridge, surely a voyage around the globe would be amply repaid by a Sunday spent in this valley.[4]

Ko Tha Byu's ministry lasted only twelve short years, from 1828 to 1840. He was already advanced in age when he was converted and began his labors for Christ. Often he was handicapped by illness and had to turn back from his tours. But he laid a solid foundation upon which succeeding missionaries and native evangelists could build. At the time of his death, there were 1,270 members belonging to Karen Baptist churches, scattered over a large area in dozens of villages. But that was just the beginning of a great spiritual movement which was destined to produce one of the most thriving of Younger Churches in southeast Asia.

In 1928, at the time of the centenary celebrations, the Karen Baptist Church was able to report a membership of 65,000, with a total Christian constituency of about 135,000. The handful of Christian workers had increased to 220 ordained pastors, assisted by 2,500 lay preachers and teachers. There were 25,000 pupils in 600 or more Sunday Schools. There were 950 schools including seven high

[4] *Ibid.*, p. 18.

schools, scores of middle schools, and hundreds of primary schools. Practically every one of the 900 odd churches was self-supporting. About two hundred Karens had gone forth as missionaries to other areas—to the wild tribes of upper Burma and across the border into China, and to the Karens and negroid tribes living in the Andaman Islands. In Bassein stood the impressive Ko Tha Byu Memorial Hall, built at a cost of $160,000, with an auditorium seating 1,500 people and a pipe organ costing $22,000, played by a Karen Christian!

Today there are approximately 200,000 Christians in the Karen churches, organized into approximately 1,900 congregations, almost entirely self-supporting—a glorious tribute to this humble servant, whom God chose to be one of the builders of his Church in the land of Burma.

2
Chi-oang and Do-wai of Taiwan

ONE OF THE most unlikely individuals to become a builder of the Church in the Far East was an elderly tribeswoman on the beautiful island of Taiwan. Despite her lowly estate, she became God's chief instrument in one of the most amazing spiritual movements in the history of modern missions.

A mountain range running the entire length of Taiwan from north to south, with peaks reaching to 12,000 feet, forms the main topographical feature of the eastern section of this island. These hills are inhabited by aborigines of the country, known collectively as the Highlanders, constituting nine different tribes with a total population of 210,000. The main groups are the Amis (86,000), the Paiwans (41,000), the Taiyals (30,000), the Bununs (20,000), and the Sediqs (14,000). The smallest tribe is the Saisets, with only 860 persons. Each group has its own language, customs, dress, and culture, but all are animists by religion.

The origin of these Highlanders is shrouded with mystery, but anthropologists generally agree that they are a Malay-Polynesian people who came to the island from southeast Asia, possibly from the Philippine archipelago or Indonesia, about the year A.D. 200. Similarity in the languages of these separated areas gives support to this theory.

For centuries these tribal peoples were the sole inhabitants of Taiwan. At first they dwelt on the fertile plains but were gradually driven into mountain fastnesses by virile and more numerous Chinese immigrating from the mainland. More interested in hunting than in agriculture, the tribal people were quite willing to concentrate in the mountains. Later on, when the Chinese began penetrating the highlands in search of furs and camphor, the aborigines became desperate and started to fight back. They carried on continuous guerilla warfare against their invaders and eventually developed the practice of head-hunting as a means of revenge.

The hills people were a very primitive group and practiced several gruesome customs. Head-hunting was the test of a man's bravery and social position. The man with the most heads to his credit was the most sought-after in marriage by young girls. At the marriage ceremony the bride and groom knelt together on a scarlet cloth in the presence of the village elders and simultaneously drank the blood of the victims from two cups hanging from the ends of a long, narrow wooden tray. When someone died, the body was smoked and dried and kept on a shelf along the wall of the home.

After the Japanese took over the island of Taiwan in 1895, they made a serious attempt to establish control over the Highlanders. They constructed a 360-mile fence, for the most part electrified, to surround the mountain regions and kept a standing army of 5,000 to patrol the tribes. The toll which the Japanese paid for pacifying the mountaineers was the loss of approximately 10,000 soldiers over the period of half a century.

Eventually, the Japanese succeeded in persuading the tribesmen to give up the practice of head-hunting. The last known instance occurred during a brief rebellion in 1930, when the Sediqs attacked a large group of Japanese and beheaded 134 of them—men, women, and children. The spirit of these tribal people is illustrated by the fact that a large number of wives committed suicide so that their husbands would not be hampered by concern for their safety, and by the fact that, when defeated by the Japanese troops, the Sediq warriors, rather than surrender, leaped to their death from a mountain path into a river gorge.

The Japanese established a good number of village schools in the mountains and sought to impose their language and culture upon the tribes people. Shinto shrines were built in every village and people urged to attend. Free exercise of their own religion was granted, but any change to another religion, such as Buddhism or Christianity, was frowned upon. Thus the Japanese government, during the entire period of their occupation of Taiwan, steadfastly resisted evangelization of tribal people by Christian missionaries. Even Japanese evangelists were forbidden to preach among them.

But God had his own plans for building his Church among these people. All this time he was preparing someone from within the ranks of the Highlanders to become the messenger of the cross to her own people.

God's instrument in this case was a woman named Chi-oang (pronounced Ji-wang), born in 1872, the daughter of a Sediq chief. The Sediqs lived mainly around the Taroku Gorge, near Hualien. Just two years after the Japanese took over the island, when she was twenty-five years of age, a Taiwanese trader selling rifles arrived in her village one day. When the man fired a shot from one of the rifles as a demonstration, the onlookers fell back in amazement, determined to possess this "strange new weapon" at any cost. The result? Chi-oang was bartered to the stranger for a handful of rifles. Thus, unwillingly, she went to live with her Taiwanese husband down on the plains. This marriage, however, was short-lived. A few years later Chi-oang's Sediq sweetheart waylaid and murdered her husband. By this time she had become adjusted to Taiwanese culture and had learned to speak both Taiwanese and Japanese. Also she had made her first contact with the Christian faith from her mother-in-law who was a Christian.

Shortly afterwards, Chi-oang married another Taiwanese, also a merchant, and traveled with him to the more prosperous western plain. During visits to Chang-hua she made further contacts with Christians.

About this time, the Sediq tribe was locked in conflict with their Japanese invaders, whom they resisted most fiercely and tenaciously. Twelve years after the occupation of the island by the Japanese, the Sediqs were still unconquered. As a last resort, the Japanese were prepared to set fire to the Taroku hills and burn out the whole Sediq tribe. Into this tense situation walked brave little Chi-oang. Able to speak both Japanese and Sediq and having an understanding of both cultures, she was able to serve in negotiating peace between the determined Japanese government and the defiant Sediq tribe. Thereafter wherever she went she was known as the woman who made peace—"Chi-oang the Reconciler." She was respected not only throughout her own tribe but also among Japanese officials.

In recognition of her service, the Japanese gave Chi-oang a plot of ground in addition to several gold necklaces, bracelets, and earrings. They also permitted her to operate a trading post in the Sediq mountains. This she managed very successfully, until her rapacious husband ran off with all her profits and gold jewelry. Stranded with her children, Chi-oang retired to Hualien, a port on the east coast near the Taroku Gorge.

In 1924, Mr. Waterwheel Lee, a preacher of the Presbyterian Church in Hualien, heard a woman sobbing in a back room of the church. It was Chi-oang, lonely and penniless, disheartened over her tragic and unsuccessful life. She listened eagerly as Mr. Lee told her of God's love and of salvation in Christ. She began to attend church services regularly and to receive further instruction in the Christian faith. Finally, at the age of fifty-two, she was baptized and joined the Church. Immediately she began to witness with great joy, telling everyone about the new peace she had found in Christ. When her Taiwanese neighbors mocked her and called her a "savage," she said to them bravely, "You call me 'savage'? It is you who are savages, for you refuse to accept the Savior."

At a synod meeting of the Presbyterian Church held at Tamsui in 1929, the question of the evangelization of the hill tribes arose once again. For years the church leaders had longed and prayed for the salvation of those Highlanders, but always the door seemed shut in their faces. Suddenly Pastor Lee remembered Chi-oang, now five years old in the Christian faith. Describing her conversion and zeal for witnessing, he asked the members of the synod, "Could it be that God wants to reach these tribal people through one of their own?"

After much prayer and thought it was decided to send Chi-oang to the Woman's Bible School at Tamsui for training in the Bible and personal work. When she was approached, she demurred at first. She was now a grandmother, fifty-seven years old, and would feel out of place among the young students. Furthermore, she was very sensitive about the tattoo marks on her face, which would set her apart from the other students, all Taiwanese. Finally, persuaded by the missionary, the Reverend Mr. James Dickson, she agreed to join the school and became a quiet but diligent student for the next two years. Upon completion of her studies in 1931, she was sent as a missionary to her own tribe under the auspices of the Women's Missionary Society of the Presbyterian Church of Taiwan.

Chi-oang immediately went up into the mountains to tell her Sediq people about Christ. When the Japanese authorities, however, discovered her objective, they ordered her back to the plains. But Chi-oang was not lacking in courage and initiative. She settled in Kaleoan, a village at the mouth of the Taroku Gorge, not far from Hualien. Sediq men came down from the mountains in the evening and waited until dark to slip past the Japanese guards. Chi-oang served the group a hot meal of rice, purchased with money donated by the Missionary Society, and then spent most of the night in instructing the men in the rudiments of the Christian faith. They left before dawn, so as to get back to the mountains before they were seen by the police. Chi-oang traveled all up and down the coast, teaching and encouraging the believers. Many times she was saved from the police by the devotion and ingenuity of her friends.

Meanwhile, God raised up a second leader for the evangelization of the Highlanders in the person of a young man named Do-wai. While serving as a room-boy in a Japanese police station near Hualien, Do-wai attended an evangelistic meeting at a Chinese Christian church and later joined its Bible class. His teacher, recognizing his ability, urged him to enroll at the Theological College in Tamsui. When his application to leave the mountain territory was denied by the police, he slipped away without permission and turned up with his wife at Tamsui, where the Reverend Mr. Dickson gave them living quarters in the basement of his house and arranged a special course of study for him.

Do-wai studied for two years, then was baptized and

returned to his own people as a Christian evangelist. Disregarding the warning from Japanese officials, he went back into the mountains, visiting relatives and friends, speaking of his newly found faith, and holding meetings secretly after midnight. While aging Chi-oang was working quietly in the region around Hualien, youthful Do-wai made extensive trips far into the central mountains. Carrying the gospel from clan to clan, he soon created groups of believers scattered widely over the mountains.

When war broke out in the Pacific in 1941, Taiwan became a point on the front line of battle. All foreign missionaries were forced to leave the island. Christians became suspected as foreign spies. The mountain people came in for special attention. Wherever Japanese police discovered Bibles and hymnbooks—even though they were in the Japanese language—they confiscated and burned them publicly. Do-wai was arrested and thrown into prison along with some of the converts who themselves became volunteer evangelists.

Japanese policemen mercilessly persecuted those Christians whom they succeeded in capturing. One of their favorite methods of punishment was to beat prisoners on their ears until they were rendered deaf and could no longer hear the good news of the Christian message. Some captives lost their minds through torture and were placed in cages and exhibited in public as a warning to other would-be converts. Several of them were put to death.

This persecution, instead of making the tribespeople renounce their faith, made them all the more determined to continue in it. If the Japanese were so afraid of the Christian God, he must be the Supreme God, a God worthy of their devotion and loyalty. They continued to meet and pray in secret, in caves and on the mountainsides, with sentries posted to warn them of the coming of the Japanese. Chi-oang was carried "piggy-back" by young men over the mountains and smuggled down the railway to escape the police. The more the military government tried to stamp out the Christian flame, the more brightly it burned. She continued to teach and pray with her disciples all during the war, under increasingly difficult conditions and severe persecution.

Her pupils had two things in common: first, they all went back to teach others and to win them for Christ; second, they all met hostility and opposition from the police. The gospel was carried from convert to convert all through the hills and hundreds were added to the kingdom of Christ. The Christian flame burned still brighter.

Chi-oang taught her people to study their Bibles and to pray daily. She urged them to work diligently at their studies and not to run off to preach before they thoroughly understood their new faith. One young man said that Chi-oang ordered him to refrain from preaching until he had studied for at least three months.

"Did you obey?" someone asked him.

"No," he replied, "I couldn't wait that long. Before I had completed my studies, I had won twenty-five people to Christ."

This is the kind of faith that moves mountains!

The end of the war found Chi-oang an aged and infirm woman but with rich rewards for her service. There were about four thousand believers among the Sediqs, who began coming down the mountains by the hundreds, knocking at the doors of little churches along the foot of the mountains and asking to be prepared for baptism. In spite of their physical deprivation and hunger, the first thing they asked for was not bread, but Bibles. Chi-oang was too feeble to travel any longer, but believers came to her from far and near, seeking her guidance and instruction. She had the joy of knowing that her beloved people had been set free from persecution.

Chi-oang died in the spring of 1946 at the age of seventy-four. Over her grave the Sediq Christians erected a monument to her memory. The Reverend Mr. Dickson visited her grave two months after her death and wrote of that experience: "This grave is indeed a sacred place for thousands who looked up to her as their spiritual mother. None in Taiwan and few anywhere else have been used of God to accomplish so much in such a short period of time." [1]

Once the war was over and Taiwan restored to the Republic of China, the door to evangelization of mountaintribes was flung wide open. Missionaries were permitted to return in even larger numbers and for the first time were able to visit the mountain areas and preach to the Highlanders. Christians were free to preach openly, and Christianity spread like wildfire. From the center of the wartime movement in Hualien, larger areas of the territories of the Sediqs, Amis, and Tayals were soon covered. In a few more years, the Good News reached into every tribe in all Taiwan, even to the Yamis of Orchid Island, forty miles off the south-east coast. Old Shinto shrines erected by the Japanese were torn down, while churches made of bamboo and thatch began to appear in scores of communities. Poor people built these churches entirely by themselves, giving of their substance as well as their labor. Self-educated lay preachers with Japanese Bibles and hymnbooks took charge of the worship services.

Some moving stories are told in connection with the building of these mountain churches. Mrs. Lillian Dickson, Presbyterian missionary, preached in a certain mountain church, and about a month later she was invited to take part in the dedication of another church still farther on. Mrs. Dickson asked, "But where did they hear the gospel?"

"Don't you know?" came the answer. "They were outside the windows of that church a month ago listening to your

[1] James Dickson, *Stranger than Fiction,* p. 13.

message, and they believed and went home and built a church!"

In the village of Cailaking a church building was erected by only ten Christian families. One of the men was extremely poor, yet he had his own house pulled down and used its beautiful beam for the new church.

In one place the church was completed, but it lacked a door. One of the Christians took the door of his own house and put it on the church. It was unthinkable to him that his house should have a door while God's house lacked one.

Do-wai was released after seven years of imprisonment and worked as a preacher, despite physical weakness, until his death in 1958.

Today, it is estimated that over fifty percent of the High-landers have accepted Christ. In some mountain villages, ninety percent of the population are Christian. The Presby-terian Church alone numbers 70,586, comprising 397 con-gregations and preaching stations, of which 110 are self-supporting. This amazing growth has been rightly described by many as a "twentieth-century miracle" or a "Pentecost in the hills."

On November 29, 1961, the Chi-oang Memorial Church was dedicated to the glory of God, with leaders of the Presby-terian Church and friends from all over Taiwan present at the service. Most important of all, the service was arranged and conducted by the ordained ministers of the newly formed Sediq Presbytery, and a choir of Sediq young people sang Chi-oang's praise in a tribal melody. The church overlooks the Taroku Gorge and stands beside a cave where Chi-oang met secretly with many inquirers during the period of perse-cution. With its high white cross, the stone edifice stands as an honorable memorial to this devoted and faithful servant of Christ, who was "the Mother of the Taiwan Tribal Church."

II
Administrators

*"If a man desire the office of a bishop,
he desireth a good work."* I TIMOTHY 3:1

As THE YOUNG church develops, new problems arise and new demands are made. To the task of evangelism must be added that of organization and consolidation. The trailblazer now gives place to the administrator. This requires men with special gifts, academically qualified as well as spiritually mature. It requires individuals with keen insight and proper judgment, able to command the respect of the whole Church.

The Younger Churches, as genuine products of the Spirit, have not been lacking in the gifts of the Spirit. To some of their members has been given the gift of administration. Samuel Crowther and V. S. Azariah are convincing illustrations of this fact.

3

Bishop Samuel Crowther
of Africa

AT THE TURN of the nineteenth century, the slave trade was
at its height on the continent of Africa. Europeans from
several lands, Arab traders, and even African chiefs were
engaged in the traffic in human lives. Though in some quarters
there was growing opposition to such trade, it was not until
the middle of the century that it was finally eradicated.

The country along the Gulf of Guinea in West Africa
constituted one of the major centers of the slave trade at
that time. Popularly known as "the slave coast," for many
years it furnished the slaves which supplied the markets of
the world. To meet this growing demand for slaves, the
country was kept in a continuous state of warfare; chiefs
contracting to furnish the slaves, making raids upon neighboring tribes and, it is said, not infrequently swooping down
upon their own villages.

The usual plan was to make the attack at night, set fire to
the humble homes, then seize and bind the inhabitants with

heavy chains, killing those who offered resistance. The captives were then joined together in a long line and driven like cattle from the smoking ruins of their homes. Thus in one night a large village would be completely destroyed. If any on the long march fell exhausted under the load of the galling chains, or an infant became troublesome, they were either killed on the spot or left to perish in the forest.

Such were the conditions in the year 1821, when very early one morning, in the flourishing village of Oshogun in Yorubaland (now western Nigeria), a sudden cry raced through the narrow lanes, "The Arabs are coming! The Arabs are coming!" Before the startled people had time to prepare, their enemies were upon them. The women fled with their children into the jungles, while the men made a desperate attempt to drive back the intruders.

Among those who sought a hiding place on that fateful morning was a young lad about fourteen years of age, Adjai, along with his mother and two sisters. But they had not gone far before they were caught by the rope nooses of the traders and led away with other captives to the town of Iseh'i, a few miles distant. The father was one of the brave men who died trying to defend their families. When they arrived at Iseh'i, Adjai and his older sister were separated from their mother and from each other. The mother and baby sister were given to the chief of the town of Dahdah, and the two older children were assigned to different people in Iseh'i itself.

For the next few months Adjai was dragged to many market towns and sold by one owner to another, often in exchange for a supply of rum and tobacco. During this period he became so despondent that he tried several times to strangle himself, but he never seemed able to muster sufficient courage to pull the rope tight enough. After several months he reached a trading town on the coast, where he was

sold to some Portuguese slave-traders. His owners put an
iron fetter on the neck of each of their slaves, forced a long,
heavy chain through each of these fetters, and fastened the
chains at both ends with a heavy padlock. Men and boys
were chained together and thrust into a damp dungeon with
no windows. The men, being stronger than the boys, would
draw the chain in such a way as to ease themselves of its
weight, with the result that the fetters were pressed against
the boys' necks so brutally that they almost suffocated, and
their necks were a mass of bruises.

Finally, when the owners had secured enough slaves to
make a shipload, one hundred and eighty-seven of them
were herded into the hold of a Portuguese steamer. Young
Adjai was utterly miserable from fright and seasickness. But
his days of misery were almost over, for Providence never
intended that he should spend the rest of his days as a slave.
God had other plans for him.

On the very day that the Portuguese slave ship set sail,
it was intercepted and captured by a British man-of-war,
H. M. S. *Myrmidon.* Captain Leeke treated the slaves with
kindness and took them all to Sierra Leone, on the west coast
of Africa, where young Adjai was put in the care of some
English missionaries of the Church Missionary Society.
Here in the mission school at Bathurst, he was taught to read
and write and was trained in the art of carpentry. From the
very beginning he proved to be an apt and avid scholar. After
four years of instruction under the tutelage of the Reverend
Mr. and Mrs. Weeks, Adjai became a Christian and was
baptized on December 11, 1825, receiving the name Samuel
Adjai Crowther.

Just at that time the Church Missionary Society established the Fourah Bay College in Freetown, for the purpose
of training young Africans to be missionaries among their
own people. The new convert, Samuel, became the first student

to be enrolled in this institution. The principal described him as a lad of uncommon ability, steady conduct, a thirst for knowledge, and indefatigable industry.

After his graduation, he was invited to remain on in the college as a tutor, and while filling this position he continued his studies, including Latin and Greek, and also worked during his leisure hours as an assistant to one of the missionaries.

While here he was married to a young African teacher whose early experience had been similar to his own. She too had been captured by the slave-traders in West Africa, rescued by a British warship, and taken to the same kind friends who had trained him. She and Adjai both came from Yorubaland and spoke the same dialect. When baptized, her name Asano was changed to Susanna. The marriage was a very happy one, blessed with six children, three of whom were later engaged in full-time Christian service.

In 1841, the British Government decided to send an expedition up the Niger River in the hope of counteracting the slave trade by establishing commercial relations with African chiefs. When officers of the Church Missionary Society learned of this enterprise, they requested permission for Samuel Crowther to accompany the party as their representative, in order to explore the possibility of establishing a mission station in that region. The request was granted, and the young tutor of Fourah Bay College was given the honor of going on that famous expedition. The journey, however, proved to be a costly one, for a deadly jungle fever attacked the party and claimed several lives, so that they were forced to return before their mission was completed.

But for the missionary society it was not an entire failure. By his tact and wisdom in dealing with the people, Mr. Crowther succeeded in establishing friendly relations with the chiefs of several tribes. Also, during the voyage he used his

leisure time in preparing a grammar and dictionary of the
Yoruba language, which afterwards proved to be of great
value. But perhaps the most important result of the expedition was that it established clearly in the minds of the
Society leaders that they must emphasize the training of
African missionaries to their own people, for they had seen
that there were parts of Africa in which the foreigner could
not live and keep his health.

Samuel Crowther, as tutor and evangelist, made such an
impression upon his missionary colleagues and his companions
of the expedition, that many of them wrote enthusiastic
letters to England about him, telling of his ability, his
modesty, and his earnestness, and recommending his ordination as full clergyman in the Church of England. Consequently, Mr. Crowther was summoned to England in the
fall of 1842 and enrolled at Islington Church College for a
year of study in preparation for the ministry. He took his
final examination under Dr. Schofield, Professor of Greek at
Cambridge, and passed with honors. Dr. Schofield was among
those who had held the theory that the mind of a Negro is
incapable of logical reasoning, but after examining Samuel
Crowther he completely changed his view and was gracious
enough to admit it publicly.

Immediately upon his ordination, the Reverend Mr.
Crowther returned to Africa, eager to begin the work of an
evangelist to his own people. He spent the days of the ocean
voyage in beginning a translation of the Bible in the Yoruba
language. The African Christians were anxiously awaiting
his arrival, for they felt that a new day had dawned for
Africa in the ordination of a member of their own race. They
referred to him affectionately as "our black minister," and
thronged to hear him whenever he preached.

The Reverend Mr. Crowther's first major appointment
upon his return to Africa was to accompany a little group

of English missionaries to establish a Christian mission at Abeokuta in his own country, Yorubaland. This was a large fortified town where several thousand escaped Yoruban slaves had formed a prosperous colony. Chief Sagbua cordially welcomed the missionary party and sent the town crier through the streets to summon a public meeting. When all the people were gathered, the Yoruban evangelist addressed them in their own language, telling them why the missionaries had come and what they hoped to do. His audience responded most enthusiastically and every one present promised a generous gift for the church building. Work on the new structure was begun almost at once, and the missionaries received so many offers of help that they could not possibly use all the eager applicants.

It was shortly after his arrival at Abeokuta that one of the most tender and moving scenes in the life of Samuel Crowther took place. By accident he learned that his mother and younger sister, from whom he had been separated for almost twenty-five years, were living in a nearby town. Concerning the happy reunion with his mother he wrote in his diary:

We grasped one another, looking at each other in great astonishment, big tears rolling down her emaciated cheeks; she trembled as she held me by the hand, and called me by the familiar names with which I well remember I used to be called by my grandmother, who has since died in slavery. We could not say much, but sat still, and cast now and then an affectionate look at each other, a look which violence and oppression had long checked; an affection which had nearly been extinguished by the long space of twenty-five years. My two sisters who were captured with us are both with my mother. Thus, unsought for, after all search for me had failed, God has brought us together again, and turned our sorrow into joy.[1]

[1] C. C. Creegan, *Great Missionaries,* p. 132.

His mother became Samuel Crowther's first convert at Abeokuta and was baptized by him, taking the name of Hannah. She was a faithful Christian right up to the time of her death at the age of ninety-seven.

The mission at Abeokuta was blessed with great success, in spite of terrible persecution by Juju priests and continuous wars waged by the king of Dahomey and his chiefs. After three years, Samuel Crowther was able to report a regular weekly attendance of five hundred, about eighty communicants, and nearly two hundred candidates for baptism. A flourishing school had been established, and plans laid for extending the work in the Yoruba country.

After working in Abeokuta for five years, Mr. Crowther felt it necessary to make another brief visit to England. He had an interview with Lord Palmerston, the Foreign Secretary, in which he explained the political situation in West Africa and laid special emphasis on the damage being done to civilization and commerce by the king of Dahomey, an African chief who was an unscrupulous slave-trader and had caused much harm to the peaceful people of Abeokuta. Lord Palmerston was so impressed with Mr. Crowther's report and appeal for help, that he made arrangements for him to appear before Prince Albert and present his case in person. During the interview in Windsor Castle, the Queen made an unexpected brief appearance and asked Mr. Crowther many questions about his country and work. The African evangelist's children used to listen with breathless interest to their father's story of his experience that afternoon.

Upon his return to Africa, Mr. Crowther resumed his ministry at Abeokuta, working in his leisure hours on the completion of his translation of the New Testament into Yoruba. In 1853, he was invited to accompany another government expedition up the Niger River, similar to the one on which he had gone twelve years previously. This at-

tempt was much more successful than the first and opened
the way for a third expedition in 1857, which proved to be
the real beginning of missionary work along the banks of
the Niger.

On this trip (which extended for 300 miles up the river),
Mr. Crowther was accompanied by a group of Christian
workers from Sierra Leone. Wherever the government representative established a trading post Mr. Crowther opened a
mission station, leaving behind one of the African evangelists.
They were cordially received everywhere, and after two and
a half years of work, several very successful centers had
been established, all of them in the entire charge of African
missionaries.

Henry Venn, General Secretary of the Church Missionary
Society, was so impressed with the success of this new
missionary venture on the Niger, that he felt the time was
ripe to appoint a bishop to oversee the work of the young
African missionaries in the newly opened stations. Faced
with the inadequacy of funds and the difficulty of the climate,
Mr. Venn took a bold step and decided that the Niger project
should be an African mission, under an African bishop. In
spite of strong opposition from some of his missionary colleagues, he recommended to the Archbishop that Samuel
Crowther be consecrated as Bishop on the Niger. Consequently, the African evangelist was summoned to England, and
on June 29, 1864, before a large and illustrious gathering,
he was consecrated to his new office and became the first African Bishop of the Anglican Communion.

The famous cathedral at Canterbury has seldom been so
crowded as on the day when, along with two other English
candidates, the "Minister from Africa" was consecrated
bishop. Special trains were run from London, and long before
the service began, thousands were thronging the building.
The personal friends of the bishops-elect were accommodated

in the chancel within a few feet of the communion rails. Immediately behind the Negro candidate sat a venerable lady who for almost forty years had weathered the climate of Sierra Leone—widow of the late Bishop Weeks. She was one of the missionaries at Freetown who had welcomed the young slave boy whom Captain Leeke, of the British man-of-war, had brought to them. She was the one who had taught him the alphabet and the Lord's Prayer. And Admiral Sir H. Leeke was there, dressed in his immaculate naval uniform, eager to witness the conferring of this great honor on the boy whom he, as a young captain, had rescued from the hold of the Portuguese slave ship so many years before. The entire country was interested in what was taking place in Canterbury Cathedral that day. The newspapers gave the event full coverage on their front pages.

Just before his consecration as bishop, Mr. Crowther was honored by the conferring of the Doctor of Divinity Degree by the University at Oxford. His Yoruba grammar, Yoruba and English dictionary, and Yoruba versions of many books of the Bible were cited as evidence of his linguistic talent and scholarly ability.

Upon his return to Africa, Bishop Crowther took up residence at Lagos, from where he supervised the work in the Niger Delta and up the river, three hundred miles to the Bida. Much was made of this mission by the Church Missionary Society. It was an experiment which aroused considerable interest. Its expected success was to be an eloquent answer to those who were disparaging the Negro race. The Niger, with its African staff and leadership, was to prove that educated Africans could carry the gospel successfully to the interior of their own continent.

The new bishop threw himself into his work with characteristic zeal and dedication. He spent several months in each year away from home, visiting the mission stations already established and founding new ones. Gradually he was able to enlarge his staff; he obtained Negro catechists and schoolmasters from Sierra Leone, posted them at different stations, and ordained those who seemed most promising. By 1871, he had ordained eight of this class of men, including his oldest son, Dandeson, who had been to Islington College in England for training. Later, Dandeson was made an archdeacon.

For more than a quarter of a century Bishop Crowther traveled among his people, strengthening and developing work already begun, building up churches, starting schools, encouraging commerce and agriculture, preparing dictionaries and grammars of various dialects, making translations of the Bible, training and ordaining new Christian workers, and lending a hand wherever there was a need. He was as skillful in teaching the people how to make sun-dried bricks as in preparing translations of the Scriptures.

The task of the African Bishop was not an easy one, for the Niger was not without dangers to his person. On one occasion Bishop Crowther was kidnapped by a hostile chief and held for ransom. The British consul at Lokoja, Mr. Fell, tried without success to secure his release, and then decided that they should make a dash for freedom. As the consul was returning to his boat, he called to Bishop Crowther to run for it too. They shoved off amid a shower of poisoned arrows, one of which struck Mr. Fell who died within a few hours. The Bishop was greatly distressed over this tragedy and later wrote to the mission secretary that he was sorry he had not been shot instead of Mr. Fell.

There were many other difficulties to be faced. Travel was exceedingly hard and tiresome. There were long distances to be covered, much of it on foot. On the river, transport was irregular and in the hands of traders who were not interested in passenger service. This made supervision of the Christian work more and more sporadic, especially as the work expanded, and kept African workers in relative isolation not conducive to the development of their spiritual life. There were constant rumors of grave irregularities in the conduct of many of the men, but Bishop Crowther could do little to clarify the situation.

During the latter years of Bishop Crowther's Episcopate, there were commercial struggles between European traders on one hand, and African merchants on the other. On the middle Niger, African ministers were closely related to, and therefore sympathetic with, the local merchants. They publicly opposed European trading houses. In the Delta area, Christians, along with their pagan neighbors, were middlemen who were being squeezed out of trade. In this struggle, English missionaries sided with their English compatriots in business.

Then there were complex cultural problems. The Niger area encompassed a wide variety of tribes, speaking many different languages and dialects and practicing a variety of customs. The situation was further complicated by the presence of many Muslims with their separate religion and culture, demanding an entirely different approach from their animist neighbors. With the exception of three or four local ministers, Bishop Crowther had to work the area with Yorubas from Sierra Leone. These men were, for all practical purposes, foreigners; they had to study the language and adjust to foreign customs. The Bishop himself had to rely much of the time on incompetent translators who greatly hindered his effectiveness.

In spite of these difficulties, Bishop Crowther was able to lay some good foundations for the Church in the Niger Delta. His mission penetrated farther inland than any other on the west coast, and was the first to meet Islam advancing from the north. Hundreds of Africans received the message of Christ and, in spite of severe persecution and trials, remained faithful to their Lord and Church. Some chiefs were converted, and with their financial backing many schools were established. Portions of the Scriptures were translated into a few of the prevailing languages, including Hausa, Ibo, and Nupe.

Much of this success was due to the leadership of Bishop Crowther himself. He was a faithful and pious Christian, dedicated and untiring in his work. He was a man of humility, always reluctant to accept high position and authority. He was a gifted linguist, skillful in preaching and writing. His tact in dealing with people won the respect of both Christian and non-Christian. Though he was very westernized in many ways and regarded himself as a "black Englishman," he never seemed to lose contact with his own people and always felt at home with them.

The greatest success of the Niger Mission took place in two sections of the Niger Delta, given the ironical names of Bonny and Brass by the English traders. Bonny was just the opposite of what its name implied. It was a dismal, swampy area with oppressive climate, infested with all sorts of poisonous reptiles, plagued with malaria and yellow fever. The moral condition of the people matched the physical surroundings. Human sacrifice, cannibalism, and infanticide were some of the prevailing practices. Religion included a strange reverence for snakes and lizards, particularly the iguanas, which were counted as "juju" (sacred), and were allowed to roam about and feed undisturbed on the poultry of the place. A large part of the population of Bonny consisted of the slaves of a few wealthy chiefs. One of these had the titular rank of king, but this honor gave him little power over the rest.

In 1864, shortly after his consecration, Bishop Crowther paid a visit to Bonny and opened a school and a "house of worship." A Negro schoolmaster from Sierra Leone was placed in charge of the work, but a few years later, Dandeson Crowther, the bishop's son, took over the mission station. The bishop himself visited the area frequently and preached the Good News of Christ to the people. In the course of time the preaching had its effect, and many turned from their paganism and evil practices and accepted Christ as the Lord of their lives. They deserted the shrines, cut down the "juju grove," and killed many of the iguanas.

Then came a period of severe persecution, led by jealous juju priests. The Christian slaves of pagan masters suffered most cruelly, for they had no means of protection. Many were beaten, imprisoned, starved, or tortured; some were killed. But nothing could stamp out the little Christian communities. One poor slave in prison received word from his master that he would not only receive pardon but also gifts and promotion if he would give up his faith in Christ, but that if he remained a Christian he would be terribly tortured. He sent back word: "Tell the master I thank him for his kindness. He himself knows that I never refused to perform duties required of me at home. But as regards turning back to heathen worship, *that* is out of my power, for Jesus has taken charge of my heart and padlocked it. The key is with Him."

The work in Bonny grew. Congregations of a thousand people assembled Sunday by Sunday in the newly constructed St. Stephen's Church. Daily family prayers were conducted in many principal compounds. It is no wonder that one of the catechists wrote with pardonable exaggeration, "Bonny has become a Bethel!" Today Bonny constitutes the Diocese of the Niger Delta in the independent land of Nigeria.

From Bonny the work soon spread to the Brass River, one of the mouths of the Niger. In 1867, the king of this section, Ockiya, welcomed the bishop and agreed to bear half the expense of a house and school for a teacher at his port, Brass-

Tuwon. Later, another school was opened in the chief town, Brass-Nembe, thirty miles up the river. The moral condition of the people here was comparable to that of the people at Bonny. The chief "juju" was the boa constrictor. The Christian message soon had its influence, however. As in Bonny, many of the people turned from their idols to the Living God. Two leading chiefs were baptized, and a few years later King Ockiya himself handed his idols over to the bishop and publicly declared himself a Christian.

Neither difficulty nor opposition was able to deter Bishop Crowther from his task. Neither old age nor illness was able to retire him. When he was called to lay down his work on earth, he was busily engaged in translating the Prayer Book into the Hausa language and was just about to set out on a trip to one of his mission stations. On December 31, 1891, he went to be with his Lord. He was about eighty-four years of age.

A historian of the Church Missionary Society says about this faithful servant of the Lord:

Few men have been at the head of a harder enterprise than Bishop Samuel Crowther; few have had more disappointments and trials; few have shown so indomitable a perseverance; few have borne through a long and laborious life so irreproachable a personal reputation. He may not have been possessed of the highest spiritual gifts; but he was a plain, practical, patient, hard-working Christian man. He suffered greatly by the faults of others. Had he been supported in Africa by men as good as himself, and in England with more constant and sympathetic counsel, his work would have been greater. Even as it was, God blessed it.[2]

---

[2] Eugene Stock, *History of The Church Missionary Society,* II, 464.

4

Bishop V. S. Azariah
of India

AMONG ALL THE great leaders whom the Younger Churches
have produced in this century, none has been greater than
Vedanayagam Samuel Azariah, first Indian bishop of the
Anglican Church in India. Other leaders have been equal to
him in one way or another; few, if any, have been endowed
with so many and such varied gifts. Azariah had at the same
time strong faith in God, a deep inner spiritual life, great
abilities as a teacher and leader of men, and vision and
courage. It was the combination of all these qualities that
made him the man he was.

Samuel was born on August 17, 1874, at Vallalanvilai in
the Tinnevelly District, South India, where his father,
Thomas Vedanayagam, was the village pastor. His ancestors
belonged to the Nadar caste in Hinduism and were tree
climbers by occupation. Though not numbered with the
outcastes, the Nadars were considered so low in the social
scale by their Brahman neighbors that they were excluded

from the right of worship in the Hindu temples. However, when Christian and government schools began to develop in the area, the Nadars seized the opportunity of an education and became one of the most virile and rapidly rising groups in India. Thousands of them became Christians, and under the influence of the gospel they have produced many leading men and women.

A Christian home and Christian teachers were the chief forces in the molding of young Samuel's character. His father had been converted from Hinduism to the Christian faith in his boyhood, and later was ordained as a minister in the Church Missionary Society. He was a simple, earnest, godly man, who practiced what he preached. His mother was a devout Christian of Spartan character, who spent much time in Bible study and prayer. Although Samuel was her only son, she never gave in to the temptation to spoil him. She had the rare gift of combining tenderness and love with discipline and order.

As a boy, Samuel Azariah attended the Christian high school at Megnanapuram, four miles from home. This was the site of an ancient temple built by his Nadar ancestors for their own private worship. When the gospel message came to the town and the last man in the community had become a Christian, the men of Megnanapuram with their own hands tore down the temple and in its place erected a fine stone church to seat three thousand. The threshold of the church, over which the new Christians entered to worship, was the old altar stone upon which they formerly offered animal sacrifices to their god.

The headmaster of the high school was a remarkable man, both an excellent scholar and a fine Christian. In his teaching he laid great stress on the right use of words and an accurate understanding of their meaning, a lesson which was invaluable to Azariah in his future ministry. Above all, he inspired in his students a great delight in studying the Bible, a joy which Azariah carried with him through life.

Thus blessed with a wholesome Christian environment, Samuel Azariah early in his youth found Christ as personal Savior and Lord, and developed those spiritual disciplines that are essential to a growing Christian life.

Samuel received his further education at the college of the Church Missionary Society in Tinnevelly and later at the famous Madras Christian College. The principal of the latter, Dr. William Miller, was a splendid Christian gentleman who deeply influenced Samuel for full-time Christian service.

Upon graduation from college, Azariah joined the staff of the Y.M.C.A., which he served for more than ten years, first as Traveling Secretary and then as Associate General Secretary. During this time he was married to a fine young Christian woman who became a perfect helper to him both in his home and in his work. Mrs. Azariah was an educated and intelligent woman, deeply devoted to her Lord and the Church. Four sons and two daughters were born, bringing great happiness to the parents. Three of the sons, a minister, doctor, and agricultural expert, served the Church faithfully for many years.

His work for the Y.M.C.A. brought Samuel Azariah into contact with Sherwood Eddy, also a secretary of the Association, and this friendship proved of great value to both young men. Azariah was able to help Eddy to understand the Indian mind and to identify himself with the people of India in a remarkable way. He sympathetically but unsparingly corrected the young American in all his mistakes of adjustment with servants and fellow workers. At the same time Eddy was able to help Azariah understand the Western mind and demonstrated that it was possible for Indian and Westerner to be friends on equal terms. Azariah learned that to disagree with a friend, sometimes to find fault with him, is not disloyalty but a sign of true friendship. So Azariah came to see that it was possible to respect the older missionaries for their devotion and work, and yet at the same time disagree with them concerning policies and methods. This lesson proved of great value later on when he became an administrator of the Church and had many missionaries working under him.

As Azariah traveled all across India and Ceylon as Secretary of the Y.M.C.A. he became increasingly burdened about the evangelization of his own people. He called to mind his own mission where there were 54,000 relatively prosperous and educated Christians in the churches of Tinnevelly, who had been signally uplifted by the gospel in every way, but who were doing practically nothing to pass on the gospel to others. One night, after a meeting in Jaffna, Ceylon, he went out under the palm trees along the seashore to pray, and there with tears he poured out his heart before the Heavenly Father. Suddenly a way of action became clear.

Upon his return to India, Azariah gathered together the young men of the churches in his home district, and after a period of prayer and consultation, they organized the Indian Missionary Society of Tinnevelly on Feb. 12, 1903. The specific object of this society was: "To develop by an indigenous organization the missionary spirit of the native Church in order to spread the Gospel in India and other lands."

The following April, a man named Samuel Pakkinadhan was sent as the first evangelist of the society to work in a hitherto unoccupied field among the poorest outcastes in the Telugu country, with headquarters near the little railway station of Dornakal, in the former Hyderabad State. On August 3, 1906, the first converts were baptized—twenty-three adults and thirty-three children. In addition three hundred inquirers were under instruction.

But even this heroic effort did not satisfy the burning heart of Samuel Azariah. An intensive study of the Government of India Census of 1901 revealed to him the disturbing fact that a hundred million people in India were utterly beyond the reach of any existing Christian agency. By correspondence with the principal mission boards in Britain and America he learned that they could not possibly open new missions to reach these unevangelized sections of India.

Azariah and his colleagues next issued "A Call to Indian Christians," and as a result seventeen delegates, speaking eight different languages and representing every part of India, Burma, and Ceylon, assembled at the historic Serampore College in Northeast India and organized the National Missionary Society, with Raja Sir Harnam Singh as president, and V. S. Azariah as general secretary. Now as secretary for both of the new indigenous missionary societies, Azariah traveled unceasingly across the country, preaching this new missionary crusade, with all India as his pulpit, calling on the students to dedicate themselves to Christian service and the churches to give their offerings for the support of the work.

Azariah naturally became more and more possessed by the missionary spirit until at last he felt called to become a missionary himself. Against the earnest pleadings of his friends, he relinquished the general secretaryship of both societies in 1909, offered himself for ordination by Bishop Henry Whitehead of Madras, and shortly afterwards, along with his consecrated wife, went as a humble worker to the wilds of Dornakal in Hyderabad State, under the auspices of the National Missionary Society. Their first home was a tent surrounded by a stockade to keep leopards and other wild animals at bay. They lived among an illiterate people who spoke Telugu, a totally different language from Tamil, their mother tongue.

Sherwood Eddy, after a visit to the area, described the people thus: "The outcastes of Hyderabad seemed to me so debased, so sunken almost in savagery, the men such drunkards and thieves and the women so stupid, that no great fruitage, no adequate results could be expected in our lifetime." [1] And yet it was among this people that Azariah, the evangelist and churchman, was to lead and mold one of the most successful and spiritual movements to Christ that the Church in India has ever witnessed.

The movement in the Dornakal area had already begun before the Reverend Azariah's coming, but he joyfully threw himself into it with all his heart and mind. He took as his slogan, "Every Christian a Witness," and whenever he baptized a new convert, he ordered the candidate to place his hand on his head and repeat the words of the apostle Paul, "Woe is me, if I preach not the Gospel of Christ." It was chiefly through the work and witness of the village lay Christians that the movement grew and gained in momentum. Within two or three years there were a few thousand converts, and a number of congregations in a score or more of villages.

The new movement toward Christianity soon attracted the attention of the Anglican authorities and more particularly that of Bishop Whitehead. It became increasingly apparent that Samuel Azariah, the leader of the movement, was a man of great spiritual gifts as well as unusual administrative abilities. His participation at the great World Missionary Conference at Edinburgh in 1910 had also brought him recognition in another sphere. Out of the 1,300 delegates present at the conference, only eighteen were from the Younger Churches. One of those eighteen was Azariah, and he was chosen as spokesman for the group. Speaking with

[1] Sherwood Eddy, *Pathfinders of the World Missionary Crusade,* p. 147.

deep feeling on the subject of the relation between missionaries and their national colleagues, he ended his speech with these challenging words:

Through all the ages to come the Indian Church will rise up in gratitude to attest the heroism and self-denying labors of the missionary body. You have given your goods to feed the poor. You have given your bodies to be burned. We ask also for *love*. Give us *friends*.[2]

To some the words seemed a bit unfair, but they did serve to remind missionaries and mission boards all over the world that the time had come to recognize their national colleagues as equals in status and partners in service.

For some time it had been recognized that the enormous diocese of Madras required an assistant bishop. The missionary bishop of the area, Henry Whitehead, felt strongly that the time had come when an Indian should be lifted to this position, so he recommended the Reverend Azariah for consecration as Bishop. At first there was strong opposition from both missionaries and Indian clergymen, the latter objecting that this honor should go to a man of low caste origin, but the idea gradually gained acceptance. The Metropolitan, however, very wisely insisted that the first Indian bishop should have a diocese of his own, however small, and a title, to prevent the growth of the idea that the natural position for an Indian bishop was that of assistant to a European. So it was decided that a new diocese should be created from the Dornakal Mission; and that in addition the new bishop should help Bishop Whitehead in the Telugu-speaking areas of the vast diocese of Madras.

Accordingly, on December 29, 1912, Vedanayagam Samuel Azariah, aged thirty-eight, was consecrated Bishop of Dor-

²V. S. Azariah, *Christian Giving*, p. 15.

nakal in Calcutta Cathedral, all eleven Anglican bishops of
India being present, along with Dr. John R. Mott, Dr. Sherwood Eddy, and other leading Free Churchmen. Ten days
later he began the administration of his tiny diocese, with
six Indian pastors and about eight thousand Christians.

Bishop Azariah's great gifts soon became apparent both
in his own diocese and in the share which he took in the episcopal work of the diocese of Madras. Gradually, the whole of
the administration of the Telugu area passed into his hands,
until in 1922, by action of the Synod, it was formally transferred to the Dornakal Diocese. When, in 1930, the Anglican
Church in India became an independent Church, Azariah
found himself bishop of a diocese as large as England, with
at that time more then 100,000 Christians under his care.

Several factors contributed to the success of Bishop
Azariah's ministry. These were related either to his particular background, his personal endowment, or his wise policies.

In the first place, having been born and brought up in a
simple village setting, he was able to understand the mind of
the villager and to adjust to rural life. Azariah had great
faith in his village people. He saw them not as what they had
been or were, but as what they could become by the grace of
God. He believed that, no matter how simple and ignorant
they were, they could be effective witnesses for Christ. For
this reason, he added to the three promises usually made by
the candidate for confirmation—renunciation of evil, promise of faith, promise of obedience—a fourth promise: to be
a faithful witness to Christ. His philosophy was: Whatever
a convert knows, little though it be, he must go and tell it
to someone else, and then come back for more. Besides emphasizing the regular day-to-day witness, the Bishop also inaugurated an annual "week of witness," which took place
during the hot season when there was not much work in the
fields. Thousands of Christians went out into the surround-

ing villages to tell of what Christ had done for them. One year over 34,000 men and women participated in the program, visiting over 3,000 villages and enrolling 7,250 inquirers. The great "week of witness" is still observed in Dornakal Diocese to this day.

Then again, having come out of a great people movement in Tinevelly District, Bishop Azariah was well acquainted with the psychology and principles of group movements. He realized that the gathered colony approach—baptizing individuals one by one and forming a Christian compound—led to social dislocation and a ghetto mentality. The group approach—baptizing whole families and leaving them in their cultural surroundings—avoided these ill effects and made for a more indigenous Church.

Thus Azariah did not hesitate to accept groups of people, small or large, as they professed faith in the Lord Jesus Christ. While some missionaries and Indian leaders trembled at the thought of receiving large numbers of ignorant and dirty outcastes into the fellowship of the Church, on the grounds that this would forever close the door to the higher castes of India, Azariah welcomed them and even rejoiced in their conversion. He sincerely believed that the Christian faith should not be judged by the type of people who accepted it, but by the type of people it produced. His position proved eventually justified, for as the high-caste people became aware of the wonderful transformation in the lives of the outcastes, their respect for the gospel began to increase. When drunkenness gave way to sobriety, quarreling and evil speech to the singing of hymns, and disorder to harmony, they began to ask questions and try to find out what it was that brought about such remarkable changes. In the course of time, over 10,000 people from the higher and middle castes professed faith in Christ and entered the fellowship of the Church.

Azariah had natural gifts as a teacher, and much of his ministry was carried out through the work of teaching. He believed that the simplest villager could understand the Bible, and that he must receive instruction from the Scriptures if he was to conduct himself as a Christian. Before a Confirmation service, he always spent much time with the candidates, instructing them in the basic teachings of the Christian faith and helping them to see the responsibilities and privileges of the Christian life. At the same time he attached the greatest importance to conferences for the clergy and teachers. He established a Divinity School at Dornakal, at which all the clergy were trained. He devoted much time and thought to this training, gave lectures himself, and had an intimate personal knowledge of each student. A printing press was also set up, which his daughter later directed.

One of the Bishop's major contributions was in the writing of several books. He usually wrote in his own language, Tamil, because of greater freedom in expressing his thoughts, and then left the work of translation to others. He wrote short studies on a number of books of the Bible and treated such practical problems as Christian marriage and Christian giving. His style of writing was lively and reflected his own faith and experience; everything was seen in relation to the needs of the Indian Church.

Bishop Azariah knew well that much of the treasure of a people's memory is to be found in their songs. Even if the villagers cannot learn the gospel by reading it, they can learn it by singing it. Rather than importing translated Western hymns, he encouraged the writing of songs and lyrics in the language and music of the people. Fortunately, Telugu is a beautiful language and the Telugu people among the most musical in India. Over the years there developed a great body of Christian songs on the life of Christ and various aspects of the Christian life. The Canticles at Morning and Evening

Prayer were rewritten in Indian style and sung to Indian tunes. Plays and dramas on Bible subjects were composed and acted in the villages. The gospel thus communicated in meaningful forms captured the hearts and minds of the village people.

Azariah was very wise in insisting that the new churches of his diocese face the problem of self-support from the very beginning. He knew well the ill effects of the mission continuing to subsidize salaries of the local pastors year after year. Such a policy undermines the principle of stewardship and stifles the spiritual growth of the people. A church that is always receiving and never giving can never achieve spiritual maturity. The missionaries had felt so sorry for the poor people that they never asked them to give. Consequently they never learned to give. Bishop Azariah was sure that all this needed to be changed. To deepen spiritual motivations for giving he added indigenous methods of giving. He urged the women, whenever they cooked, to put aside a handful of grain for God. Each week they brought their bags of grain and offered them in the church. He suggested that those laborers who received daily wages should set apart a small amount each day and bring their offerings to the Sunday service. To the farmers he suggested that they consecrate their first-fruits to the Lord—the first eggs, the first calf or lamb, etc.—and that at the time of harvest they give a generous thanksgiving offering for the work of the Church. In these ways, gifts that seemed small at the time, over a period of weeks and months amounted to quite a large sum.

Another factor which contributed to the growth of the Dornakal Diocese was the Bishop's wise policy in the use of his personnel. He put his leading Indian clergymen in charge of the churches and schools and evangelistic work in the villages, and he used his missionary staff to take over many of the details of supervision. Working in close cooperation with

the Bishop, they relieved him of all the business side of the
diocese, such as finance and administration. They watched
over the clergy and dealt with many problems that otherwise
would have come to the Bishop, thus setting him free to do
the work which only he could do. In addition to this, Azariah
encouraged the idea of "a village ministry for village people,"
a policy which the pioneer Welch missionary, the Reverend
John Thomas, had developed in the original people movement
in the Tinnevelly Diocese. Azariah took faithful men who had
served effectively in the villages, even though their educational qualifications were low, and ordained them as full-
fledged pastors. When he took over the diocese in 1912, there
were only six Indian clergymen in his fellowship; when he
died in 1945, there were more than a hundred and fifty.

Without doubt, however, it was the inner spiritual life of
Bishop Azariah that made him such an effective minister of
God and builder of the Church. He was accustomed to rise
very early, usually before five o'clock, and spend a long time
in prayer before beginning the tasks of the day. This was a
discipline that he had learned both at home and at school in
his youth. He kept a list of all the workers in his diocese and
prayed for many of them each day. To devotion he added
knowledge. Besides being an incessant student of the Bible—
of which he memorized many portions—he made a careful
study of the best books in English and even acquired a fair
knowledge of Greek. Long train journeys and quiet evening
hours were seized as opportunities for reading and study.

Commenting on the spiritual life of Samuel Azariah,
Bishop Stephen Neill, a colleague, wrote: "To the end,
Azariah was really a very simple man. To him, Jesus Christ
was Savior and Lord; it was his one aim to be made like Him.
The whole purpose of his life as Bishop could be summed up
in the words, 'That God in all things may be glorified.'" [3]

[3] V. S. Azariah, *Christian Giving*, Introduction by Stephen Neill, p. 18.

It was no small achievement that the Bishop was able to implant this same spirit of devotion in the hearts and minds of many of the village Christians. All the new converts and, as far as possible, all members of the Church either personally observed a daily quiet time of Bible study and prayer or, if their educational level was not yet up to this, met every evening in the churches to study the New Testament and to pray. Dr. Sherwood Eddy, who visited the diocese often, estimated that nearly a hundred thousand met each evening and some twenty thousand each morning for such services throughout the diocese. Each Christian was taught that he was a living witness and a voluntary worker, and no man was paid as a professional evangelist to preach the gospel.

One of the happiest days in the life of Bishop Azariah was January 6, 1939, when the new Cathedral in Dornakal was consecrated. Gifts for the building had come in from every part of the world. In keeping with the Bishop's love for Indian culture, the Cathedral was built in an Indian style that combined elements of Hindu, Muslim, and Christian architecture. Bishops and outstanding churchmen from five different continents and a vast throng of Indian Christians from all over the district were present for the grand occasion. Fifteen hundred communicants took part in the service of Holy Communion. It was a glorious tribute to the remarkable ministry of the first Indian bishop of the Anglican Church in India.

Azariah's influence extended far beyond the borders of his own jurisdiction. For years he served as the chairman of the National Christian Council of India, Burma, and Ceylon. At the Lambeth Conferences people listened to him with affection and respect. In 1938, at the Tambaram meeting, he was appointed one of the six vice-chairmen of the International Missionary Council. Cambridge University conferred upon him the honorary degree of Doctor of Laws. He traveled far and wide—in Europe, the United States, and Australia—and wherever he went, his life and ministry made a profound impact. The village pastor's son from Vallalanvilai had become one of the greatest and most honored leaders in Christendom. But in his heart he remained the simple village boy, unspoiled by the glamor of position and acclaim of the world.

Perhaps Bishop Azariah's greatest contribution to the Church in India was the part he played in laying the foundation for church union. From an early time, he was a strong critic of Western denominationalism and an ardent advocate of Christian unity. He said that in the West denominationalism may be a weakness, but in the East it is a sin. At the Edinburgh Conference on Faith and Order, he said to the group: "To the older churches of the West, Christian unity may be a matter of secondary importance, but to the younger churches of the mission field, Christian unity is literally a matter of life and death." [4]

In 1919, Azariah was present at a famous conference of Indian ministers at Tranquebar, which sent forth a challenge to all the separated churches in India. From then on until the time of his death, he served on the committee which was trying to formulate a plan of union to bring the Anglican, Presbyterian, Congregationalist, and Methodist Churches together into one great fellowship. It was a difficult task, and all Azariah's statesman-like qualities were needed to prevent the scheme from being wrecked on the rocks of denominational conservatism and national pride. Alas, he did not live to see the day, in September 1947, less than three years after his death, when the Church of South India came into being. But the achievement owed a great deal to his wisdom and patience, and the

[4] Eugene L. Smith, *God's Mission—and Ours*, p. 124.

members of the C.S.I. will long remember the one who was among the greatest of its builders. The union of Churches in South India inaugurated a new era for the universal Church: the door was opened for similar advances toward unity in other parts of the world.

The last years of Bishop Azariah's ministry were clouded with difficulty and sadness. Many of his old friends had died or had left India. The work of the diocese presented new problems. It became increasingly difficult to maintain the spiritual glow of the early days when everything was new and the people movement was at its height. Christians of the second and third generations have a tendency to lose the enthusiasm of their fathers who made the original break with paganism. To them Christianity becomes a matter of inheritance and not of personal choice. They present a new set of problems which demand new methods of approach. The Bishop found himself less at home with these young people than he had been with their grandparents; often he was rather severe in his judgment on them. Some of the educated members became more and more critical of the Bishop's paternal methods of rule, which had been quite suitable for the early days of the movement; they demanded more democratic patterns of church administration. In addition, the long delay in achieving church union was often frustrating to the Bishop; he became less patient and more prone to pass judgment. It was clear to all that the Bishop was growing old.

In spite of all these difficulties, Bishop Azariah was happy in his work and full of energy right to the end. During the Christmas season in 1944, he went out as usual to visit the village congregations which he loved so dearly. He became ill with a fever and returned home, fully expecting to be up in a few days. However, the long years of labor had taken their toll; he had no strength left to throw off the illness.

On New Year's Day, 1945, at the age of seventy, he quietly passed away.

All day long, thousands of village Christians came to pay their final respects to the man who had given them spiritual birth and had so faithfully nurtured them in the faith. In the evening they laid him to rest in the garden of the great cathedral that he had built.

When Samuel Azariah was consecrated Bishop of Dornakal, there were 50,000 Christians in his area, including the Telugu-speaking Christians in that portion of the Madras diocese for which he was responsible. At the time of his death, there were close to 250,000 Christians in the Dornakal Diocese, making it the largest diocese of the Indian Church. Whole communities had been delivered from their former degrading practices and lifted to a new level of living. Hundreds of churches dotted the countryside. There were thousands of schoolchildren who met in worshiping congregations each Sunday.

Samuel Azariah stands as a glorious example of what God can do through a humble servant who is utterly dedicated to his Lord, who is burdened over the spiritual needs of his people, and who is willing to put first things first.

III

Evangelists

*"And he gave some, apostles; and some,
prophets; and some, evangelists."* EPHESIANS 4:11

YOUNGER CHURCHES, LIKE older Churches, constantly face the
danger of losing their first love. The initial burst of enthusiasm
tends to give way to complacency. Second- and third-generation
Christians are prone to look upon their faith as a matter of
family heritage, rather than one of personal commitment. Religion becomes more of a label than a life.

At such times of spiritual declination, the Lord often raises
up evangelists to help revive the Church and call her back to
her primary mission. They are usually men of deep spiritual
experience, with natural gifts of persuasion and discernment.
They may be homespun like Tamil David or brilliant like John
Sung, but they are fully surrendered to Christ and have a genuine concern for people.

5

Tamil David
of India

TAMIL DAVID[1] WAS born in an obscure village called Komma-
dikottai, in Tinnevelly District, South India, in 1853. His
parents were Christian workers in the Church of England
mission field. His father died when David was just two years
old, so at an early age he was sent to the mission boarding
school. Perhaps from the want of a father to discipline him,
the boy grew up to be very mischievous and obstinate, causing
his mother and teachers a great deal of trouble. Besides his
uncontrollable temper, he was dishonest and disobedient and
had an adverse influence on his fellow students. Once he was
dismissed from school for breaking one of the rules, but the
principal had pity on him and received him back. But shortly
afterwards David, sixteen years of age, ran away to Ceylon.

For about a year Tamil David was able to meet expenses

---

[1] His initials were V. D., but his full name is not known. He was
always called "Tamil David," Tamil being the name of his native language.

by teaching in a small primary school. Then it happened that an Australian came to Ceylon and opened up a grand liquor store. He could neither read nor write, and looking about for someone who could keep the accounts for the store, he decided to engage the services of young David. He started David on a small salary but gave him the entire management of the money. The temptation proved too much for the wayward young man, and soon he was helping himself freely to both the funds and the liquor supply. He began to wear fine clothes, frequent the theater and billiard halls, and give himself over to a life of excitement and pleasure. Later he went into partnership with a Singhalese and the two started a liquor shop of their own. Business was good and David made still more money.

Meanwhile Tamil David's mother grieved much over the waywardness of her son, but she kept on praying for his conversion. When David was about twenty-three years of age, she went to Ceylon in search of him and persuaded him to return home with her to India. Shortly after this, she made arrangements for David's marriage to Mary, a mission-educated girl and sincere Christian. David never set eyes upon her until they stood before the church altar to take the marriage vows, but according to his later testimony, as soon as they came out of the church and talked together for the first time, he was quite pleased with his mother's choice.

On the other hand, Mary was greatly disappointed when she discovered that her husband was not a sincere Christian. Within three hours after the marriage ceremony she brought a tract and urged him to read it. David felt insulted and angry over the incident and threw the tract away. On many occasions he was rude to his wife as she tried to conduct family devotions, but she bore it all in loving patience and kept praying that God would change his life. Often David did not return home until the early hours of the morning, but she was always waiting at the door to meet him with a smile.

At the end of a year David returned to Ceylon, taking Mary, and opened up another liquor store. His wife's heart almost broke over this action, but she remained patient and sweet, taking all things to God in prayer. Her exemplary life and tender love had its effect, however, and at last David closed his liquor shop and decided to become a teacher in the mission school.

One day as he was walking down one of the streets in Colombo, it seemed as if he heard a voice saying, "David, you are wrong." It made him extremely miserable, and for days he could hardly sleep or eat. He knew there must be something in the Christian life which would satisfy his heart, but he did not know how to find it. He tried to read tracts and the Bible, he tried to pray, but still he was not satisfied. He shared his burden with his wife who kept telling him, "You must believe, you must believe." But what was he to believe, and how was he to believe?

What followed is perhaps best told in Tamil David's own words:

For some time I continued in this troubled state. I found some relief in praying and reading the Bible, but I still longed for something I knew not how to find. I was like a firefly flitting about in the darkness of the night. I read many tracts also, but neither they nor people were finally instrumental in showing me the light. It was a verse I found in Romans 4:5 that finally led me to Christ. The meaning of the verse is: "Not to man that worketh, but believeth, to him it will be counted righteousness." The Holy Spirit brought that verse to my heart in a forcible manner. I had been working all this time to find salvation. I stopped working. I simply sat still and ceased trying to save myself by my own efforts. I began to believe just what God said; I took Him at His Word. Suddenly peace broke into my heart. The burden was rolled away. I began to shout at the top of my voice. Away I ran to a public street and began to bawl out: "Sinner, come to Christ! Sinner, come to Christ!" [2]

Tamil David became a changed man by this personal confrontation with Jesus Christ. The boys in the school soon noticed the transformation, but most especially did his wife. There was a new spirit of love and harmony in the home. Husband and wife now began to eat and speak and hold family devotions together. The former habits of smoking and drinking were miraculously broken. A desire to preach the gospel took hold of him.

Things went quite well with Tamil David for a few months, but then he seemed to hit a snag in his spiritual life. Though he preached often, except for an occasional convert there were no real results in his service. He became discouraged when people laughed or threw stones at him when he preached in the open air. His work and preaching became a duty rather than a privilege. His spiritual life was more like pump-work than a flowing river. There was no overflowing joy in it. Though he had been delivered from the sins of the flesh, the sins of the spirit now seemed to plague him. To put it in his own words, "The lions and tigers and elephants of sin were turned out of my heart, but the little foxes, ants, and flies still remained to annoy me." Especially was he defeated by an ill temper that was the bane of his life.

From this state of despondency David sought release by seeking to make restitution for all his old debts, some of which had been standing since he was nine years of age. With the help of his wife he paid them all off. It took him four years. But still he felt he was not the deep Christian he

[2] *Life of Tamil David*, pp. 10-11. Published by The Bible Warehouse, Madras, India.

ought to be. His ministry was a duty and not a delight. He longed for something more.

It was a Salvation Army captain who was to become the means in God's hand to lead Tamil David into a deeper and more effective Christian life. The man was not well educated, but his life was radiant and full of power. He was not an eloquent preacher, but his life spoke more effectively than his words. His spirit of joy was contagious. He spoke to David about the work of the Holy Spirit in a Christian's life. "My dear David," he exhorted, "why don't you consecrate yourself fully to the Lord, and then He will use you wonderfully."

He led David to an upper room in his house, left him there alone and closed the door on him. "Stay there," he commanded, "until the transaction is complete."

Later David described what happened to him in that upper room:

I began to consecrate my life wholly to God. I made an unconditional surrender. I yielded my all, especially my will. One by one the Lord brought the following questions into my mind. "Are you willing to give up your job if asked to do so?" I answered, "Yes." "Are you willing to go to Africa for the sake of the Gospel?" That was hard, but I replied, "Yes." "Are you willing to leave your wife and go to other lands alone, if called?" Ah, that was very hard, but I was in real earnest and answered "Yes." I was willing to put God first and everything and everyone else second. Then all struggle ceased. All my life was on the altar. I was willing now to do anything, to go anywhere.[3]

David waited then for some visible manifestation, but none came. He felt disappointed.

Finally, another question arose in my heart. It was this: Have I been cleansed from all evil? I hardly thought so, for the

[3] *Ibid.*, p. 16.

preachers had told me that evil remains more or less in our hearts all our lives. I knew the Bible says all filthiness of the flesh and spirit must go, but I had never taken possession of the truth. Then I remembered the verse: "The blood of Jesus Christ cleanseth from all sin." I immediately took God at His word and believed the promise. By simple faith I received what I had been longing and striving for, for so long: the Holy Spirit or the life more abundant. I did not feel anything extraordinary, but I knew the Lord had full possession of my heart. I got up and went home without any feeling.

The next day was Sunday. I went to church still feeling nothing, but never for a moment doubting that Christ dwelt in me. After the sermon by the pastor, God put it into my heart to go up and speak to him. I said to him, "The Lord gave me last night the life more abundant, the baptism of the Holy Spirit." As soon as I said that, his face lit up and my heart was filled with fire. I didn't know whether I was standing on my head or feet. I felt as if I had six wings to fly. I hardly knew when I reached home.[4]

That evening David had charge of a small service at his home as usual. It was the same message, but a new preacher. His words seemed to be fraught with unusual power. The people started weeping, then they began to shout the praises of God. Great joy came upon them all.

From that day it was evident that Tamil David's life was lifted to a new plane of effectiveness. Discouragement gave way to optimism, defeat to victory, and ill temper to a spirit of meekness.

At the same time David's innate abilities were quickened and his whole ministry vitalized. His preaching took on a new urge and power and began to bear immediate fruit. When he witnessed to people on the street, they knelt then and there and surrendered themselves to Christ. Once

---

[4] *Ibid.*, pp. 16-17.

he spoke to a "devil dancer" (a sorcerer, or one who practices black magic) whom he met as he was walking along. The man immediately fell on his face and cried to God for mercy. He promised that he would burn all his books of magic and go out to witness for Christ to his people.

When David preached in the churches, conviction seized the congregation and many repented of their sins and turned to Christ for salvation. A genuine revival broke out among the Singhalese around Colombo, and scores of people were converted. In a boys' and a girls' school where he conducted meetings, many of the students found Christ as their Savior.

However, life was not easy for Tamil David after his "upper room experience." Just as the people of Jerusalem began to mock the early disciples on the day of Pentecost and say that they were drunk, so some of the nominal Christians began to criticize David and call him a mad fanatic. The elders even tried him for heresy and cast him out of the Anglican Church. The evangelist bore it all in Christian love. Later, when these same people began to see how God was using David and blessing his ministry, they received him back into the Church and welcomed him to their pulpits.

After a few years of evangelistic work in Ceylon, Tamil David was invited by the Reverend George Grubb, a British missionary, to accompany him on a preaching mission to Australia. David's ministry proved as effective there as it had been among his own people. Several hundred Australians were converted under his preaching. Next he accompanied the Reverend Grubb to the British Isles, holding meetings in England, Scotland, and Ireland. At the great Keswick Convention in England, his preaching was singularly blessed by the Lord. As a result of this extended tour, David became quite proficient in preaching in English, an accomplishment that later was to open many other doors for him in the West.

Tamil David then returned to India and there continued his evangelistic ministry for some time. Everywhere he went, revival broke out. Like a flame of fire he swept across the southern tip of India from Madras on the east coast to Cochin on the west, and then down through the state of Travancore (now Kerala) among the Syrian churches.[5]

It was here, in Travancore, that Tamil David witnessed the greatest response to his preaching during his entire ministry. On one occasion, when a large audience of about 25,000 people assembled on an open plain to hear him preach, an unusual outpouring of the Holy Spirit took place. Many stood and openly confessed their sins; others fell to the ground and sobbed like little children, crying out to God for the forgiveness of their sins. For ten days the meetings continued all day long, with only a few hours of rest in between. During the next three months it is estimated that over 10,000 people were converted. Several young men were called into the Christian ministry. One of this group was Sadhu Kochukunchoo who became a very effective evangelist among the Mar Thoma Christians. To this day his name is known in every Kerala Christian household. He was something like a second Tamil David, though his ministry was limited to a much smaller area.

The climax of these meetings in Travancore seemed to coincide with the spiritual revival that had recently given birth to the Mar Thoma Church, a reform movement within the ancient Syrian Orthodox Church of India. The preaching of Tamil David gave added impetus to this reform movement and also to the great Maramon Convention, which today is one of the world's largest annual Christian gatherings. Held on the sand bed of a river in the month of February, this

[5] The Syrian Church is one of the oldest churches in Christendom. According to tradition, this church was founded by the apostle Thomas who went to India as a missionary and died as a martyr for his faith.

week-long convention attracts anywhere from 25,000 to 50,000 people in a single service.

Once, while conducting a preaching mission in the Methodist Church at Lucknow in Northern India, Tamil David gave witness to the Holy Spirit's sustaining power which enabled him to preach several times a day without undue physical and mental fatigue. The secret, he pointed out, was to relax, keep free from tension, and draw on inner spiritual reserves. A young missionary by the name of E. Stanley Jones was sitting in the audience and gave special attention to the evangelist's witness. Broken in health and discouraged, he was facing the possibility of having to terminate his missionary career and return to the United States. Tamil David's words went straight to his heart. For the next few minutes the missionary heard nothing else that the evangelist said. In his mind he was carrying on a silent conversation with his Lord. Finally the inner voice said to him, "If you would surrender your physical problem to me, I could take care of it for you."

Quietly, with faith, he responded, "Lord, I put the problem in your hands."

At that moment the miracle of healing took place, and Stanley Jones became strong where once he had been weak, namely, in nervous energy. Today, more than eighty years old, this missionary extraordinary is still preaching two to three times a day and finding his strength in the sustaining grace of our Lord.[6]

As the fame of Tamil David spread, he began to receive invitations for revival meetings from other countries. His travels took him to such far-off lands as Malaya, China, Japan, Australia, South Africa, Italy, the British Isles, and the United States of America. While in England he was

[6] This incident was narrated to the author by Dr. E. Stanley Jones in a recent conversation.

granted an audience with Her Majesty, Queen Victoria, who gave him a seat by her side and listened with great interest as he told of his meetings in India.

When Tamil David went to Australia for meetings, he was nicknamed "Black David," and it was arranged that he should be accommodated with the cooks and menials. David cheerfully bore the insult, and he took the opportunity to preach the gospel to the cooks and to pray with them. A short while later, out from the kitchen arose the jubilant chorus of songs and praises from the lips of those cooks, and people outside in large numbers flocked to see this "Black David." Those who came to see him were touched by his sincere exhortations and invited him to speak at important gatherings. The very people who accommodated him in the servants' quarters were sorry for their prejudice and invited him to many dinners and parties where he was hailed as the guest of honor. They dropped the nickname of "Black David" and called him by his real name, V. D. David.

Mr. David's ministry in America was greatly used by the Lord to the blessing of many. The American people dubbed him as "The Apostle of the East." Once, while holding revival meetings in Trinity Methodist Church, Chicago, David was urged by Dr. Frank Crane, the pastor, to tell the congregation of the many revivals that he had witnessed in India. The evangelist hesitated to comply with the request, but when the pastor urged that the narration of these experiences would quicken the faith of God's people, David agreed to do so. Before an audience of over a thousand people, the "Apostle of India" told the marvelous story of God's transforming power in the lives of his own people. The effect was astounding. Over one hundred persons fell on their knees and cried for forgiveness or for the fullness of the Holy Spirit.

One of the young men converted here was George P. Tasker, who later became a missionary to India. He was

loaned by his own mission board to the Methodists and served
for three years as pastor of the Bangalore Methodist Church.

In the United States, Tamil David worked in close association with the world-famous evangelist Dwight L. Moody.
One year he was invited by Mr. Moody to address his Summer Conference at Northfield Massachusetts. David took as
the theme of his messages, "The Life More Abundant." In
one of the open-air meetings on Round Top, in the middle
of his message, black clouds began to appear, and there were
signs of a heavy rain storm. The people began to scatter, but
under the inspiration of the Holy Spirit, Mr. David cried
out, "Stop! There will be no rain!" He later testified that he
himself was surprised at what he said, for the words seemed
to come unconsciously from his lips. The amazing thing was
that the threat of rain instantly passed. The incident caused
a great stir in the city.

Some of the outstanding features of Tamil David's preaching and ministry are worthy of note.

In the first place, he refused to take any offerings in his
meetings so as to avoid the criticism that he was preaching
for money. He completely trusted God to supply all his
personal needs and the funds for his travels. On one occasion
the people insisted on coming and filling his pockets with
money, so that he was hardly able to walk. Later he counted
out a total of eight hundred rupees. David prayed and asked
the Lord what to do with the money. "He put it in my heart,"
he testified, "to use it to support a worker among the neglected classes of India. Now I have six native workers with
me, Praise the Lord!"

Secondly, in his preaching, Tamil David laid great stress
upon the place of the Holy Spirit in the life of a Christian.
As a result there was revival wherever he went. He insisted
that the missionaries also should emphasize this truth in
their lives. To the people of England he said, "You must

stop sending to India men and women filled with all kinds of learning but lacking the life more abundant. They make so few converts that India will never be won by their efforts. It is absolutely imperative that the first and foremost qualification of each missionary be that he or she is filled with the Spirit."

Mr. David wrote a tract entitled, "Have You the Baptism of the Holy Spirit?" A copy of this tract came into the hands of a British missionary in Uganda, the Reverend G. L. Pilkington. This young missionary had been three years on the field and done some translation work but felt keenly disappointed at the dearth of spiritual results in his ministry. So, in a mood of great despondency, Pilkington had gone for a few days of meditation and prayer to Kome, a small island in Lake Victoria. Here it was that he read Tamil David's tract and was led into the experience of the fullness of the Holy Spirit. When he returned from Kome to his mission station, Mengo, on December 7, 1893, he immediately testified to his new experience. As a result a great revival broke out in the work of the Church Missionary Society (Anglican). Christians of old standing found new power and purity; chiefs came forward and confessed that hitherto they had been only nominal Christians; and a large number of unbelievers were converted. From that time onward the work of the mission grew by leaps and bounds. The missionaries began to go out into the villages and preach. Hundreds of volunteer African evangelists went out in all directions. In the first two years, two hundred new congregations were organized. And all was the work of the infant Church without a penny of English money.

Such were the far-reaching effects of the Spirit-filled ministry of Tamil David.

Mr. David loved to preach out in the open and on the streets. Once while he was in Colombo, Ceylon, he could not get a license for street preaching. But he was not a man who would give up easily. Selecting a crowded street corner as his forum, he stood at a prominent place and read aloud portions from the Bible, so that the passerby might hear the Word of God. When the police objected to this, he argued that the rules of the state prohibited only *preaching* in the streets, not the *reading* of the Scriptures!

David often fell into step with some pedestrian on the road and walked a mile or two just to be able to witness to him about the Savior Jesus Christ. When his companion reached his destination, David, on his way back, walked with another pedestrian and spoke about the Lord. He had an all-consuming desire to share Christ with others.

Perhaps the preaching of Tamil David can best be described in the words of an Indian Salvation Army officer in South Travancore. After attending one of Mr. David's meetings, he observed,

David can be compared to an expert hunter who plays the role of a "beater" and makes the wild animals run out of their hiding places and, while they are fleeing for their lives, brings them down with a gun. David first stirs the hearts of the hearers, and when they are cut to the quick and feel so despondent trying to flee for their lives, he shows the unbounded love and message of salvation and thus "bags" the repentant sinners. A mighty hunter indeed! [7]

Many are of the opinion that there has been no preacher in India equal to him in zeal and sincerity. Sandhu Sundar Singh, North India's outstanding Christian, also testified to his greatness.

[7] *Life of Tamil David,* p. 49.

6

John Sung
of China

ONE OF THE most colorful and effective evangelists of the Christian Church in China in this twentieth century was John Sung. His ministry was short but fruitful, and the results of his preaching remain to this day.

John Sung was born in the village of Hong Check, Fukien Province, on September 27, 1901. He was the sixth child in a family of ten children, six sons and four daughters. His father, Pastor Sung, a minister in the Methodist Church, had dedicated him to God's service even before his birth. As he was the first child to be born in the home since Mrs. Sung's conversion, he was given the name of Ju-un, "Saving Grace." Later on, by popular usage, the Chinese name gave way to the familiar English name, John.

Father Sung was a man of hasty temper, and it soon became evident that his son had inherited a similar disposition. As the child grew to boyhood, there were constant clashes between him and his parents. The father used the bamboo rod freely, but young Ju-un rebelled all the more. Once, in a fit of rage, he butted his head against one of the earthenware jars standing in the courtyard, and it broke in pieces. On another occasion, in a quarrel at the breakfast table, Ju-un threw hot rice into his brother's face, scalding him and breaking the bowl.

About 1907, Pastor Sung moved with his family to the city of Hinghwa, where he was appointed Assistant Principal of the Methodist Bible School. Ju-un, now six years of age, started attending Sunday School, and the Bible stories began to make a strong impression on his mind. At the Church day school he showed signs of outstanding ability, and this brought great joy to his father.

Two years later, an unusual spiritual experience seemed to change the whole atmosphere of the Sung home and especially the life of young Ju-un. This was the great Hinghwa Revival of 1909-13. It all started when one of the women missionaries in the city wrote a letter to some friends in America with the plea, "Please pray for revival in our station." Two ladies responded to the appeal and gave themselves to intercessory prayer until they received the assurance that revival would come to the Hinghwa congregation. They were assured that this work would begin on Good Friday and wrote their friend in China to tell her so. The letter was delayed and arrived after Easter. Nevertheless, the revival had broken out, on Good Friday!

As a result of the quickening work of the Holy Spirit, the entire congregation at Hinghwa was spiritually revived and empowered. The Church became a witnessing Church, and within a month or two, three thousand people were converted. Many new chapels were built throughout the district.

Young Ju-un Sung was present that Good Friday morning when the revival broke out. He could never, all his life long, forget the service and sermon of that day. When the invitation was given, he made his way to the altar and through tears confessed his sins to the Savior. He was genuinely converted, and his life was soon marked by an exceptional love for the Word of God, an unusual desire to pray, and a passion to preach.

Pastor Sung was among those who experienced a new advent of the Holy Spirit during the revival. As a result, a new bond of love developed between father and son. The two often climbed a nearby hilltop and spent much time in prayer. Communion with God became a real joy, and together they shared the secrets of the Father's presence.

By the time Ju-un was in high school, he had developed quite a reputation as a boy preacher. "Here comes the Little Pastor," became a familiar cry throughout the area around Hinghwa, when Ju-un accompanied his father to the villages on his preaching trips. Whenever Pastor Sung was prevented from fulfilling an engagement, his young son was only too glad to substitute. Open-air preaching, distributing tracts, selling Bibles, conducting the singing, all these he loved to do.

In spite of all this, there were some disconcerting aspects of Ju-un Sung's conduct. There were still fits of bad temper, exhibitions of pride, and selfish habits uncontrolled. This led his father to the conclusion that Ju-un was not really suited to the ministry, so he decided to launch him on a naval career. However, just before time for the entrance examination, Ju-un became quite ill. By sheer dogged determination he sought to go through with the application, but because of his physical condition at the time, he failed both the medical and the written examinations.

Back at school, Ju-un gave himself diligently to his studies. He became editor of the weekly school newspaper and assistant editor of his father's magazine, *Revival*, which had a wide circulation. During the holidays and in his spare time, he devoted his energies to preaching the gospel and to con-

ducting literacy classes for country children. At the end of
his high school career he graduated with the highest marks
in his class.

One day Ju-un Sung abruptly announced to his father,
"Father, I have decided I want to go to America to study."

Pastor Sung was indignant. "Where do you think I'm
going to get the money to send you to America? I'm not the
mandarin of Hinghwa but a poor preacher."

Undaunted by the rebuff, Ju-un began to pray about the
matter. For a whole week he prayed to God to open the way.
Then one day a letter arrived from Peking. It was from an
American lady missionary who promised to secure a scholarship for him in Ohio Wesleyan University. This was wonderful, but the problem of his travel expenses was still unsolved.
However, when the pastors in the district heard of the situation—many of them were Pastor Sung's former students in
the Bible School—they began to send in their gifts in vary-
ing amounts. Soon Ju-un had more than enough to buy his
ticket to America. When his father saw this, he finally gave
his consent to the plan.

On March 2, 1920, Ju-un sailed on the S. S. "Nile" for
San Francisco. His first years in the United States were a
struggle against many odds. Loneliness overcame him. His
English was poor, and he was unaccustomed to American
ways. Widespread unemployment in the country made it
difficult to find remunerative work during the vacation
periods. He developed an abscess at the base of his spine
and had to undergo an operation. On many occasions, rather
than be financially dependent on others, he worked; washing
dishes, scrubbing floors, beating carpets, and mowing lawns.
The strain of all his problems, added to the demands of his
studies, led him into periods of deep melancholy.

In spite of this, the hand of the Lord was upon Ju-un
Sung. As a student he showed extraordinary scholarship

with a marked proficiency in chemistry and mathematics. Teachers and students alike respected this gifted young visitor from China. Dr. Rollin Walker, Professor of Bible at Wesleyan, took a keen interest in Ju-un and became one of his closest friends. On Sundays, Ju-un was in great demand for preaching. He organized evangelistic bands among the students and was their leader on preaching excursions to the rural churches.

In slightly over three years Ju-un completed his college course and graduated in 1923 with high honors. He was awarded the gold medal and the cash prize for physics and chemistry and was elected to Phi Beta Kappa. His picture with accounts of his brilliance appeared in newspapers all over the country and brought him fame overnight. The University of Minnesota at once offered Sung a post as demonstrator and assistant in chemistry. Harvard University offered him a scholarship to study medicine. Yet another offer was to study theology.

Finally Sung decided to accept a scholarship for graduate studies at Ohio State University. In June, 1924, he took his M.S. degree and was awarded the Science Society's medal and gold key. After another year and nine months he completed all the work for his doctorate and received his degree in March, 1926, before a large and distinguished assembly which showered him with congratulations and honors.

However, by this time Sung had completely deviated from his original purpose in coming to America. His prowess in chemistry, the honors that were heaped upon him, and the attractive offers that were made to him, all pushed his desire for Christian service far into the background. The urge was still there and kept tugging at his heart, but the lure of the world was too strong. As a result, Sung was in a constant state of inner conflict and unrest, which often led to periods of depression.

As he was contemplating his future, one day the Reverend Wilbur Fowler, the Wesley Foundation representative at Ohio State University, called to visit him, and in the conversation he said to Sung, "You know, you are not a bit like a scientist. You look far more like a preacher."

It was then that Sung opened up his heart and confessed the inner struggle through which he was going. At once the Reverend Fowler challenged Sung to enter Union Theological Seminary at New York in preparation for the ministry. Sung gave his consent without hesitation, and the autumn of 1926 found Dr. Sung enrolled as a student at the Seminary.

The decision to pursue theological studies, however, seemed to come more from Sung's head than his heart. His will was still unsurrendered to God. Thus the state of inner conflict continued. Moreover, the spirit of skepticism which was prevalent at the time began to shake the foundations of his Christian faith. No doubt his low spiritual condition made him an easy prey to doubt.

So he began to turn to the ancient religions of the East for solace. He read many volumes on Buddhism and Taoism. He even resorted to chanting the Buddhist scriptures in the secret of his room. He made the rounds of the many cults and theosophic societies with which New York abounds. But all in vain. The world seemed altogether meaningless and life full of nothing but misery. Describing his feelings at this low time, Sung later wrote: "My soul wandered in a wilderness. I could neither sleep nor eat. My faith was like a leaking, storm-driven ship without captain or compass. My heart was filled with the deepest unhappiness." So morbid and depressed was he at the time, that the Seminary authorities feared for his sanity.

Shortly before Christmas, John Sung accompanied some fellow students to a special evangelistic campaign at the First Baptist Church. He expected to hear Dr. Haldeman, an eloquent and learned preacher, but instead, the speaker was a fifteen-year-old girl! She spoke simply and yet powerfully. The proud, skeptical heart of the Ph.D. scientist was moved to the depths. So impressed was he, that he went back for four consecutive evenings, and each time the tremendous power in the young evangelist's preaching gripped him. He determined to discover for himself the secret of such spiritual power.

During the Christmas vacation, John Sung turned to Christian biography to investigate the secret of the effective ministry of great Christians of the past. He soon discovered that in each case it was the power of the Holy Spirit that made the difference. So he determined that he would find this power for himself. He stayed away from classes and spent the time in prayer. Several days passed.

Then one evening, light broke on his darkened soul. As he wept and prayed, he heard a voice saying, "Son, thy sins are forgiven," and all at once the load seemed to be lifted from his shoulders. With a feeling of intense relief he leaped to his feet and rushed out into the halls of the dormitory shouting, "Hallelujah!" He was conscious of the indwelling presence of Christ in his life.

The depression and gloom of the past months suddenly gave place to an unrestrained and lighthearted exuberance. John Sung sang as he walked through the halls of the dormitory; he witnessed to everyone whom he met. He put aside his text books and gave himself solely to reading his Bible. He walked up and down the corridors repeating Scripture passages to himself. He paced the floor of his room far into the night, praying aloud. But all this only confirmed the suspicions of the Seminary authorities that the years of intensive study and recent emotional strain had upset the balance of Sung's mind. So he was placed in the psychopathic ward of Bloomingdale Hospital for treatment.

Sung was given to understand that he would be kept in the hospital for six weeks only. When the time was up, he asked for his discharge, but to his dismay the request was denied. Feeling that the authorities had deceived him, he argued angrily with the doctor. His old fiery temper flared up, and the doctor, convinced that his patient was indeed mentally unbalanced, ordered him to be transferred to the ward for violent patients.

Unable to bear the atmosphere of the Ward, Sung escaped from the hospital and hid in a wheat field a few miles from the asylum. An urgent call to the police, however, resulted in his swift capture and return to the hospital. But after a week he was able to have a calm and sensible talk with the doctor and was then returned to the original psychiatric ward, where there was peace and quiet again. Sung spent a total of six months in Bloomingdale Hospital. He used much of his time in meditation, prayer, and the study of God's Word. He read through the Bible forty times and made voluminous notes from his study. God taught him many new lessons in the Christian life and gave him glorious victory over his bad temper. It was a time of genuine preparation for his ministry which lay ahead.

When Sung was finally discharged, it was on condition that he leave the United States and return to China. So on October 4, 1927, he sailed from Seattle and headed for his homeland. He had been in the United States for seven and a half years. He had earned three degrees and distinguished himself in the field of chemistry. Already several universities in China were making attractive offers to him to serve on their faculties.

Sung realized the fierce temptation he would face upon his arrival home to sidestep the call of God and enter into the academic field. One day, as the vessel neared its destination, he went down to his cabin, took out of his trunk his diplomas, his medals, and his fraternity keys and threw them all overboard except his doctor's diploma, which he retained to satisfy his father. He was determined to be obedient to the heavenly vision.

Immediately upon landing in Shanghai, Sung discarded his European clothes and donned the simple cotton gown of his homeland.

There was great rejoicing in the Sung home at Hinghwa as they welcomed back their most distinguished son. But Pastor Sung's joy soon turned to disappointment when John announced that he would not be accepting a position in some great university but was dedicating his life to the preaching of the gospel. His father had hoped that John would be able to draw a good salary and help to educate his younger brothers. However, when he saw the sincerity and determination of his son, Pastor Sung accepted his decision and gave him his blessing.

A sore trial now awaited John: his wedding. The marriage had been arranged by his parents several years previously, and now it was time to consummate the union. John accepted the inevitable, but with no joyful anticipation. He did not know the girl. He did not even know whether she was a good Christian. But the marriage proved quite successful, and Mrs. Sung became John's faithful companion through all their eighteen years of life together. Three daughters and two sons were born to them. Besides their regular Chinese names, they were also given Bible names. The first four were called, Genesis, Exodus, Leviticus, and Numbers. For the fifth child, the parents skipped Deuteronomy and chose the name of Joshua. (Exodus died in his third month. "In keeping with his name," John said, "he *went* out to be with the Lord.")

John Sung spent the first three years of his ministry serving the churches in and around Hinghwa. He devoted his time mainly to reviving the congregations in the smaller towns and villages. He was accompanied by a band of enthusiastic young men and women who gave their personal testimonies in the services, while he himself did the preaching. Everywhere they went, the meetings were characterized by a spirit of confession and repentance. Many churches and individual Christians were revitalized and renewed. Those who had been merely formal church members were converted and became living witnesses for Christ.

To strengthen the spiritual life of the village pastors, John Sung developed certain patterns of his own. First he started an itinerant theological school. Beginning with five students, he divided the time between Bible study and evangelism. The group kept on the move, studying, working, and preaching. In this way they combined experience with theory.

Then Sung worked out a plan for the systematic training of local preachers. He divided the hundred or so villages of the district into groups of ten and devoted a whole year to visiting each group in turn. At every center, forty or fifty representatives were summoned to attend classes on the Bible, family worship, and teaching methods. One result of these efforts was that family worship was started in more than a thousand homes.

In 1930, Dr. Sung joined the Hinghwa Conference of the Methodist Church and entered a wider sphere of ministry as evangelist-at-large. Invitations for special meetings came in from all over the province. In all these campaigns, God's hand lay mightily upon the young evangelist, and there were many cases of genuine revival.

Sung's reputation as a successful evangelist soon spread far and wide, and calls now began to pour in from many parts of the country. Campaigns in Kiukiang, Nanchang, Shanghai, Nanking, and Tenghsien were characterized by unusual outpourings of the Holy Spirit. In Kiukiang almost all the

Methodist High School students—about two hundred twenty —turned to the Lord during the meetings and subsequently organized evangelistic bands to witness for Christ in their spare time. In the school at Nanchang about one hundred eighty students and teachers came to Christ in confession of their sins and were added to the Church. One night in the city of Tenghsien, there were three hundred people seeking to get right with God and with one another, amid scenes of deep distress and tearful repentance.

One of Sung's most successful campaigns was held in the city of Amoy. When the largest church in town could not hold the crowds, a special mat-shed was erected to accommodate twenty-five hundred people. On one occasion, five thousand people attended a mass meeting on the football grounds of the Anglo-Chinese College. Not only were many Christians revitalized, but several notorious sinners in the city were marvelously converted. One gambling house in Amoy was forced to close its doors when it lost most of its regular customers. Finally city authorities became perturbed at the interruption of communications by the crowds attending the meetings and requested the evangelist to leave town. But the meetings went on in Sung's absence, with overflow crowds in the churches and many new conversions.

By 1934, John Sung had become a well-known national figure in the Christian world of China. He headed a list of six "notable personalities" among evangelical leaders published by the National Christian Council. His contribution to the revival which was sweeping over large parts of China was considerable. Everywhere he went, crowds thronged to hear him. People often arrived two or three hours early in order to be sure of seats.

The secret of the success of evangelist John Sung was twofold. First, his devotion to prayer. He spent much time between meetings in earnest pleading with God on behalf of cold churches and nominal Christians. Second, his intense earnestness. His preaching was impassioned and straightforward. He was not afraid to denounce sin and call people to repentance.

Sung believed strongly that there are three secrets of revival: (1) a thorough confession of sin; (2) prayer for the fullness of the Holy Spirit; (3) public witness for Christ. In keeping with the latter emphasis, at the end of every campaign he organized evangelistic bands to go out into the surrounding villages and witness for Christ. In Amoy and Kulangsu, one hundred forty-seven such bands were organized, and they visited all the villages on Amoy Island.

Sung's meetings were lively but always under control. The service began with singing, the evangelist himself sometimes conducting with the use of a white hankerchief. Often he urged the audience to clap their hands to the music. Unison prayer by the entire congregation followed. Then, after a brief prayer by the preacher, the message began. Sermons were illustrated in a variety of ways. Crude blackboard drawings and written sermon outlines were commonplace. Sometimes members from the congregation were called to the platform to help illustrate a point. Men were frequently tied up with ropes and then released to illustrate the power of sin and the deliverance which Christ offered.

In one meeting the local missionary had beautifully decorated the platform with all her potted ferns and flowers. Sung was emphasizing the necessity of pulling up sin by the roots when he spied the plants. To dramatize his point he set to work, pulling the plants up one by one and strewing them about the floor. Needless to say, there were no floral decorations the next night!

Evangelist Sung's sermons were not so much in the nature of topical development as of a running commentary on long passages of Scripture, with apt illustrations and applications. His exposition probably would have horrified some of the Bible teachers of our time. His ideas were often fanciful in the extreme. Yet he was able to introduce his hearers to the contents of the Bible and to instill in them a sincere desire to study the Word. Thus, wherever he went, the Bible societies were soon sold out of their stocks and had to wire urgently to the central depots for fresh supplies.

Sung's greatest fault was probably his slashing attacks on preachers who he felt were not faithful to their responsibility of preaching the gospel and winning people to Christ. Church officials, mission school teachers, and even missionaries came in for their share of judgment. Though at times there was some truth in his criticism, the attacks were often unwarranted and tended to alienate some who otherwise would have been his friends. However, in the latter years of his ministry, Sung's approach became much more sympathetic and kindly, which endeared him to the hearts of all.

It was inevitable that John Sung's fame as an evangelist would eventually attract the attention of the Chinese churches overseas. Calls started coming in from various places.

The first invitation came from the Philippines in 1935, with three denominations in Manila uniting in an evangelistic campaign. Each night about eight hundred people filled every seat and blocked the aisles and stairways of the Chinese United Evangelical Church. There were many converts, notably among them the Chinese consul general in Manila. He had lived a life of debauchery and sin in many cities, was a heavy drinker and an ardent gambler. Once he lost 180,000 dollars in Hong Kong money at a single sitting. Today he is the warden of a Bible college in Java, a man of whom it is difficult to believe such a history.

Right after the Manila campaign, Dr. Sung traveled to

Singapore. This turned out to be the first of seven visits to this important crossroad of the world. It was here that he conducted some of his greatest campaigns and made a lasting impression on the churches. Many of the Christians in Singapore today look back to the visits of John Sung as the time of their first real Christian experience.

From Singapore, evangelist Sung crossed over to the mainland to conduct campaigns throughout the Malay Peninsula. It is estimated that over five thousand people were converted in these meetings.

When Sung sailed from Singapore for home, the crowds to see him off were so great that the P. & O. Steamship authorities had to devise a scheme whereby the people formed a queue, filed onto the ship up one gangway, shook hands with the evangelist on the deck, and then left by a second gangway. Over one thousand people said good-bye to him in this way.

After the ship had sailed, Sung discovered to his surprise that he had an extra package in his cabin, a baby, wrapped and labeled, from an anonymous donor! The Bethel orphanage in Shanghai took charge of the gift upon his arrival there.

In April, 1936, Dr. Sung crossed over to Formosa for his first campaign on that island. Meetings were arranged in the three main cities of Taipeh, Taichung, and Tainan. In the last two cities well over five thousand made a profession of faith, and four hundred sixty offered themselves as voluntary evangelists. Four thousand dollars in cash as well as gold rings and jewelry were contributed for the support of the two hundred ninety-five evangelistic bands that were formed.

That same year, Dr. Sung conducted a great Bible conference in Amoy, from July 10 to August 9, for the express purpose of establishing the new converts in the faith. One thousand six hundred delegates converged on the city from all parts of China as well as from Singapore, the Malay States, and the Philippines. Beginning at the first chapter of Genesis, Dr. Sung took his audience right through the Bible, chapter by chapter, down to the last chapter in Revelation. Has any other Bible teacher ever attempted anything comparable? Surely this was a phenomenal effort for one man in one month! All the addresses were taken down verbatim and published in a single volume of 554 pages.

New areas began to open up for the message of this "flame from China." A campaign in Sibu, northern Borneo, was greatly blessed by the Lord. A total of 1,583 people were brought to repentance and faith in Christ. Over one hundred young people dedicated themselves to Christian service. Four young women were sent to Nanking for training. One hundred and twenty-six witness bands were formed.

In the spring of 1938, John Sung made his first visit to Bangkok in Thailand. The meetings were held in the large Baptist Church built by Dr. Grosbeck. The Spirit of the Lord was present in mighty transforming power. The following year, the Presbyterians used him for several weeks in some of the major cities of the country. In the twenty years between 1915 and 1935, the number of church members in the Presbyterian Church in Thailand had decreased from eight thousand to less than seven thousand. Two years after the visit of Dr. Sung, the membership had increased to nine thousand.

Perhaps one of Dr. Sung's greatest overseas campaigns was in the Netherlands East Indies (now Indonesia) in the year 1939. The meetings in Surabaja, Batavia, Bandung, Madium, and Solo on the island of Java drew some of the largest crowds that ever heard the Chinese evangelist and produced some of the greatest results. The campaign closed with a ten-day training school in Surabaja, attended by two thousand "volunteers" from all over the island. Using the Gospel of Mark as the basis for his Bible study, Dr. Sung instructed and prepared this splendid group for the task of evangelizing their own people in Java.

But the strenuous schedule to which Sung had given himself was now beginning to take its toll upon his health. The earthen vessel had begun to show signs of wear. His heart was none too strong and there were symptoms of tuberculosis of the hip. During his last meeting in Surabaja, he had to preach in a kneeling position to lessen the pain in his hip.

Upon his return to the mainland, Dr. Sung entered the Peking Union Medical College for a complete checkup. The examination revealed that he was suffering from cancer as well as tuberculosis. Over the next three years a series of three operations were performed, the ailing evangelist's condition deteriorating all the while.

On the evening of August 17, 1944, John felt that his end was near. He told his wife that God had shown him he was going to die. His last words to her were, "Don't be afraid. The Lord Jesus is at the door. What is there to fear?" At daybreak the next morning, at the age of forty-two, John Sung went to be with his Lord. His brilliant career as an evangelist had lasted only seventeen years, but during that period thousands had come to know the Lord as Savior, and hundreds of churches had been revived. To this day a countless number of people remember with gratitude this amazing flame for God in the Far East.

IV
Educators

"And he gave some, . . . teachers." EPHESIANS 4:11

IN THE DEVELOPMENT of the Younger Churches, education has been the partner of evangelism. Whereas evangelism has sought to produce disciples of Jesus Christ, education has sought to make them intelligent and mature disciples. At times, education has actually been the forerunner or agent of evangelism.

The Younger Churches have not been lacking for educators. Here are the biographies of two persons who were outstanding in this field. One of them had the courage to withstand the prejudice of centuries and win for the neglected women of her land the right to an education and a contributive role in society. The other had the faith to believe that education was the key to the evangelization of his fellow countrymen.

7

Pandita Ramabai
of India

PANDITA RAMABAI WAS patriot, scholar, reformer, and saint. She was small in stature—a little more than five feet in height—but a giant in spirit, towering above the women of her day. She had only one child of her own, but she lived to see the day when thousands of children lovingly claimed her as mother.

Ramabai's parents were members of the Brahman community, the highest caste in Hinduism. Both were very remarkable persons. Her father, Ananta Shastri Dongre, was a great scholar of the Hindu scriptures and the Sanskrit language. Young men flocked to study under him.

In his outlook Ananta Shastri was far in advance of his time and believed strongly in the education of women. He suffered much persecution because he taught his wife and daughters not only to read and write Marathi, their mother tongue, but also the sacred Sanskrit language, the very "voice of the gods." His fellow priests even threatened to excommunicate him for this daring breach of Hindu custom.

On the other hand, Ananta Shastri's great learning brought him widespread fame, and he was called upon to recite selected portions of the *Shastras* (Hindu scriptures) before many rajahs all across India. For this he received princely gifts of money and once even a pair of young elephants.

Ramabai's mother, Lakshmibai, was no less remarkable in her ability. Married when only nine years of age, under the tutelage of her husband she became a proficient scholar of Sanskrit and committed many thousands of the religious stanzas to memory. In time she had six children, of whom she reared three, managed servants, and entertained her husband's many students and constant guests. Besides all this, she kept a garden and supervised the care of a large herd of cattle. All her clearheaded foresight, grasp of detail, and executive power were passed on to her daughter in an even greater degree.

Because of the threatenings of Brahman priests, Ananta Shastri decided to go to live in the secluded forest of Sangumal, in western India, where his actions would not offend. The spot was so lonesome and remote that often the howls of wild beasts terrified the family in the dark hours of the night.

In this forest home on April 23, 1858, a little daughter was born, to whom the father gave the name of Ramabai—it may be translated "the delightful one"—and he determined that this little girl should have a chance for an education unhampered by Hindu customs and restrictions.

Ramabai was an eager and bright student. At the age of seven she began her study of Sanskrit, and by the time she was twelve, she knew several thousand slokas[1] of the classics by heart.

---

[1] A *sloka* is a poetical unit, in length anywhere from a couplet to a whole stanza, setting forth some philosophical or religious truth.

Not long after the birth of Ramabai, the family suffered heavy financial losses and suddenly was reduced from great wealth to poverty. This was due partly to the father's practice of lavish hospitality, and partly to the dishonesty of men whom he trusted. Ananta Shastri sold everything to pay his creditors, and the family then set out on a life of pilgrimage which took them thousands of miles up and down India over a period of fifteen years. They supported themselves by gratuities given by rajahs and students, to whom they gave religious instruction.

Finally, in 1874, during the great famine in the south in which five million people perished, both the father, now seventy-eight years old, and the indomitable little mother, only forty-seven, died within six weeks of each other of actual starvation. A few months later Ramabai's sister died of cholera.

Ramabai was now sixteen years old. She and her brother pressed slowly northward, and for a period of three or four years they wandered about, lecturing occasionally on education for women and on other ideas they had gained from their father. By this time, Ramabai estimated, they had walked over seven thousand miles since the family had started on its life of pilgrimage.

In 1878, Ramabai and her brother reached Calcutta, where they discovered, to their surprise, that her fame had already preceded her. She was invited to give her lecture before the assembled pandits of that great city, and so astounded were they by her scholarship and knowledge of the Sanskrit scriptures, that they conferred upon her the highest title possible in India for a woman—Sarasvati, "Goddess of Wisdom." Thereafter she was addressed as "Pandita," the feminine of pandit (which means "scholar"). This is the equivalent of being addressed as "Doctor" in the countries of the West.

Suddenly Ramabai was the news of the hour, and papers

all over the country trumpeted her accomplishments. All India was dazzled by her ability. She was a woman of purest Brahman birth, twenty years old and unmarried, beautiful and scholarly. She knew six Indian languages, and she could not only recite faultlessly the thousands of slokas she knew, but she had a gift for extemporizing poetry and enchanted her admirers by composing in a few minutes one sloka after another, perfect in form and full of meaning and wit, on whatever subjects they assigned her. Moreover she won the hearts of all by her personal charm and her modesty.

Pandita Ramabai received many offers of marriage from Brahmans in high positions, but she refused them all in order to care for her brother who was in ill health. Finally, in 1880, upon the death of her brother, she was married to a Bengali gentleman, Bepin Bihari Medhavi, M.A., B.L., a graduate of Calcutta University and a lawyer by profession.

Medhavi was a Shudra by caste—much lower than the Brahman—so Ramabai was almost irredeemably discredited in the eyes of her fellow Brahmans. She was, however, very happy for a year and a half, until, on February 4, 1882, her husband died suddenly of cholera, leaving her with a little daughter, whom they had named Manoramabai, "Heart's Delight."

Ramabai now suffered all the shame of widowhood which was prevalent in her day. She clothed herself in a white sari and cut her hair short, both symbols of her unfortunate state. (Orthodox custom required that the head be shaved.) As the outcaste widow of a Shudra, her position was especially despicable. Further, her husband's untimely death was interpreted in the usual Hindu manner as the result of her karma (evil deeds committed in a previous existence) and this only added to her disgrace.

At last Ramabai yielded to the urgent entreaties of her friends and went to live in Poona, in the western section of

India. Here, with the kind and courageous backing of several leading citizens of the city, she continued her lectures and soon afterward formed a society known as the Arya Mahila Samaj (literally, Aryan Women's Society), whose object was the promotion of education among women and the abolition of child marriage. She went from city to city throughout the Bombay Presidency, establishing branch societies and arousing the people by her eloquent appeals.

In Poona, Pandita Ramabai began the study of English with Miss Hurford, principal of the Government Female Training School. Though not a missionary, Miss Hurford was a sincere Christian and agreed to teach Ramabai English on condition that she be allowed to instruct her in the Bible also. Ramabai, being a born linguist, made quick progress in her language study, but the Bible lessons soon caught her main attention. The Gospels made a deep impression upon her heart and mind, and she was especially attracted by Christ's loving and courteous attitude toward women.

From then on in her public lectures, instead of quoting from the Hindu scriptures as previously, she began to quote almost exclusively from the Gospels. Without doubt, Ramabai had now begun her spiritual pilgrimage that eventually was to lead her to personal faith in Christ.

Ramabai realized that she needed further training to successfully pursue her work for the uplift of the women of India. Early in 1883, she sailed for England with her daughter, Manoramabai, now nearly two years old. Proceeds from a book she had written on *Morals for Women* furnished the money for her passage.

In England, Ramabai and her child went to Wantage, where they were lovingly received by the Anglican Sisters of the Community of St. Mary the Virgin. There she was given further instruction in English and a careful grounding in the Christian faith, and there she saw for the first time Christianity in action. One thing that impressed her was the rescue work for women as a new thing in religion, something which not only rewarded the good and virtuous, but attempted even to lift the fallen.

As a result of what she saw and heard, Pandita Ramabai was finally convinced of the truth of the Christian faith, and she and her little daughter were baptized in the church at Wantage on September 29, 1883. News of her baptism brought great joy to Christians in India, but deep gloom to her Hindu friends. To her critics it was but an added proof of her degradation.

From Wantage, Ramabai went to study in the Women's College at Cheltenham, where she taught Sanskrit to pay expenses.

Early in 1886, Ramabai received an urgent invitation from her close friend, Anandabai Joshi, to attend her graduation from the Woman's Medical College of Pennsylvania. Anandabai was the first Indian woman to receive the M.D. degree. She was a brilliant girl, not quite twenty-one years of age when she received her degree.

Ramabai intended to return to England in a few weeks, but she was soon caught up in a round of activities that kept her busy across the American continent for almost two and a half years. Between journeyings and lectures, she studied kindergarten and grade school methods, prepared a set of readers for Indian children in the Marathi language, wrote in English a stirring book called *The High-Caste Hindu Woman*, and almost completed in Marathi a book about life in the United States.

As a result of Ramabai's stirring lectures, she won many friends, and on December 13, 1887, the "Ramabai Association" was formed of enthusiastic women and several notable men, who pledged themselves to support for ten years a school to be opened in India by Pandita Ramabai for the education of high-caste widows.

With a task cut out for her, Ramabai now returned to her motherland after an absence of more than six years. She was no longer a poor, friendless widow but a leader supported by thousands of sympathetic friends both in England and in America. Within a few months, in March 1889, the Sharada Sadan (House of Learning) was opened in Bombay, and Ramabai began her work of education for the helpless childwidows in that section of the country. The following year the school was moved to Poona, where it remained for more than ten years.

In order for us to understand the real significance of Pandita Ramabai's work, it is necessary to recall the pitiful lot of the child-widow at that time in India's history.

In those days the practice of child marriage was very common. Young girls and even infants were given in marriage to older men, and often the husband died while the bride was still in her infancy. Though she had really never been a wife, the girl was considered a widow and not permitted to remarry. The death of her husband was usually attributed to her karma, and she was looked down upon by society.

The child-widow was deprived of all her ornaments, forced to shave her head completely, and wear a single course garment, white, red, or brown in color, and assigned to all the menial tasks of the home. She was not permitted more than one meal a day, and was not allowed to take part in the family feasts and community festivals.

Such was the pitiful state of the child-widow when Pandita Ramabai opened her school in 1889, with twenty-two students enrolled.

Ramabai had promised the Indian Committee of the Association that she would not seek to proselyte any of the girls in her school. It was to be strictly a nonsectarian institution.

The girls would be allowed to follow their own worship and religious rites. However, Ramabai made it plain that the Bible would be an open book in the school, and that she would not turn away any girl who desired to join with her in her daily devotions.

This agreement was followed scrupulously until the inevitable happened. One by one the girls asked permission to join their new "mother" in her devotions, until shortly the whole school was voluntarily and regularly attending. The reading of God's Word began to make a great impression upon their searching minds. Besides, Ramabai's personal charm, her wonderful example, and her warm love for these unfortunate young widows began to influence them in favor of Christianity.

During this period Ramabai herself made great progress in her own spiritual life. Ever since her baptism she had been comparatively happy to think that she had found a religion which gave its privileges equally to men and women, regardless of caste or color. But she had failed to understand that the Christian life consisted primarily of a personal relationship with Jesus Christ.

In 1891, while feeling very unhappy and dissatisfied with her spiritual state, she read a book, *From Death unto Life*, by Mr. Haslam, a minister of the Church of England. This book helped her to see her lack and to enter into a new experience with the Lord. From then on, Ramabai's greatest joy was in telling others of the wonderful salvation in Jesus Christ.

In 1894, when one of the girls asked for Christian baptism, a storm broke. Twenty girls were immediately withdrawn from the school. Anonymous letters threatened Ramabai's life; the newspapers poured abuse upon her; the Advisory Board resigned, and circulars were sent to parents and guardians urging them to withdraw their girls. It was a dark hour for Ramabai, but she was convinced that she had kept her side of the bargain and bravely stood her ground.

Of the forty-two girls left in the Sharada Sadan, most were orphans whom Ramabai had herself gathered in. Some of them she had rescued from a life of extreme cruelty. One girl used to be shut in a room filled with the choking smoke of burning peppers, or suspended from the ceiling by her wrists. Another girl was starved and beaten and often suspended through a ring hung from the ceiling. Another girl, only ten, was treated so brutally—even branded with hot irons—that one of Ramabai's committee members disguised himself as a wandering ascetic, kidnapped the girl from her guardians, and brought her to the school.

After the storm broke, Ramabai continued her work undaunted. The abusive criticisms in the papers gave her much free publicity, and the Sharada Sadan became known to many unhappy widows who otherwise never would have heard of it. After the Advisory Board resigned, more than a dozen of the girls who were of age were baptized, while others under age anxiously waited their time.

About this time Ramabai received a new impetus in her own spiritual life, which made her even more effective in her work and witness for Christ. In 1895, she read the life of Amanda Smith, an American freed slave who became an evangelist and was well known in certain circles of her day. She used to shout for joy that she had been twice delivered from bondage—from the bondage of slavery and the bondage of sin. Amanda Smith spoke much of the fullness of the Holy Spirit as the source of her joy and victory, and this sparked in Ramabai's heart a strong desire to truly be a Spirit-filled Christian.

Soon after this, Ramabai attended a Methodist camp meeting in Lonauli, and there, under the ministry of the English evangelist Mr. Gelson Gregson, she made a deeper surrender of herself to Christ and received the assurance that the Holy Spirit had taken complete possession of her entire personality.

It was in the same year that Ramabai read the stirring stories of the lives of John G. Paton, George Mueller, and Hudson Taylor, all mighty men of faith. She decided to launch out on an adventure of complete trust in God for all the needs of the mission.

By that time, fifteen of her girls had found Christ as their Savior, and Ramabai suddenly felt impelled to pray that God would square their number within a year. She then had forty-nine girls in her school, room for only sixty-five, and funds for only fifty. To take on the responsibility for two hundred twenty-five girls was indeed a leap of faith.

Within a year and a half, Ramabai's family grew in number from forty-nine to three hundred. Most of the girls were starving young widows and children, picked up off the streets, victims of a terrible famine that was then raging in the Central Province of India. There simply was not enough room for all of them in Sharada Sadan, so Ramabai took them all down to Kedgaon, a small town thirty-four miles south of Poona.

The previous year, Ramabai had bought a hundred acres of land in this town, hoping to make there a farm which would in time help to support the school. It was to this barren, stony place that Ramabai took her poor waifs. At first she put up temporary matting shelters and then, as soon as possible, suitable buildings. She dug wells, planted trees, ploughed and sowed fields, and in time made a little village where there had previously been nothing. The new school at Kedgaon was given the name Mukti Sadan (House of Salvation or Liberation).

For all this undertaking the Lord wonderfully supplied the needs, both for finances and personnel. In one year, gifts totaling 85,000 dollars came in from friends all over the world. Dedicated helpers began to arrive on the scene, both from within India and from abroad. More than a score of American and English women came to Ramabai's help, faithfully serving without salary for many years.

Of course, Ramabai's dearest helper was her own lovely and capable daughter, Manoramabai, who until her untimely death in 1921, carried an increasingly heavy share of her mother's great burden.

During 1900 and 1901, a severe famine raged in the northwestern section of India. Ramabai sent twenty of her women to the area, and they came back with 1,350 women and children whom they had rescued from the brink of starvation. This brought the total number of wards to more than 1,900.

The physical and spiritual care of this overwhelming multitude was staggering, but the little generalissima and her staff of helpers rose bravely to the challenge. Slowly order was brought out of chaos; new buildings were erected, new wells were dug, and new industries were set going. The institution never had more than 1,900 girls at one time, but altogether, from 1889 to 1922, it is probably a very moderate estimate that Ramabai must have taken in well over three thousand people. Many of the girls went out as teachers and Bible women, and many hundreds were married to Christian men.

By this time, the Ramabai Mission had developed into three separate departments—the School, the Rescue Home for fallen girls, and the Orphanage. Later a small school for orphan boys was added. The organization and management for twenty-two years of this institution—not only enormous and complex, but taxing the heart as well as mind—gave full play to an executive capacity which stands unparalleled in India. It amounted to nothing short of genius.

All this time the spiritual impact of the institution continued to grow. On October 26, 1897, seventy-three persons were baptized and soon after, thirty-six more; and so, on to the end of Ramabai's life, larger and smaller groups continued to come to Christ and into the fellowship of his Church. The rapid increase of conversions culminated in a great revival in 1905, when the fires lighted at Kedgaon spread to many churches in India and brought a new glow into many a heart around the world.

The prayer bands at the Mission grew in attendance within a few months from seventy to seven hundred, and in one year they prayed for no less than twenty-nine thousand individuals by name. Gospel teams went out from Kedgaon to many other places to conduct evangelistic meetings with similar results, while people coming to the center from distant parts carried the blazing torch to new sections where the fire of evangelism broke out and began to spread.

Not satisfied with all she did, Ramabai set up a printing press with four machines. While at Wantage in England she had learned to set type in her spare time, and now she taught her girls to set type in Marathi, Hindi, English, and later on in Greek and Hebrew. She even had them trained in running the presses and in bookbinding.

Finally, in addition, Ramabai undertook to translate the whole Bible from the original languages into Marathi, her mother tongue. She was not satisfied with the existing translation, which she felt was too stilted and pedantic. Her aim was to produce a translation in pure but simple Marathi that even the common villager could understand. She first devoted her time to a careful study of Hebrew and Greek, and then took up her colossal task with characteristic resolution. The assignment took her about fifteen years, a little every day, and she completed it only a few months before her death. When she passed away, a 50,000 copy edition of the translation was already under way. Ramabai's many friends in New Zealand underwrote the cost of printing the Bible as a memorial to her.

In 1919, the British Government honored Pandita Ramabai by awarding to her the Kaiser-i-Hind medal for distinguished service to Indian education. It was a fitting recognition of her initiative in demonstrating that the millions of widows might be educated and thus become a blessing to the community, instead of being a burden to the family and a blight on the nation.

Pandita Ramabai, tireless to the end, succumbed to septic bronchitis on April 5, 1922. She was herself to the last— alert, praying, praising God, and thinking of others. An unprecedented procession filed by her coffin all day long on that memorable day. Brahman and outcaste, rich and poor, Indian and European, all alike came to do her honor.

Ramabai was borne to her grave on the slender shoulders of some of her precious girls and laid to rest within sight of a great well which she herself had named "Dhir" (courage). It was a fitting symbol of this courageous widow, who by God's grace was one of the most outstanding women that India has ever produced.

Today the world famous Ramabai Mukti Mission in Kedgaon, with its many buildings and institutions spread out over one hundred eighty acres, stands as a magnificent memorial to this remarkable servant of Christ and of her beloved India. There are seven hundred fifty women and children now living within Mukti's portals, and all the privileges and training of a Christian home are theirs. Included in this number are orphans, unwanted babies, widows, unmarried young mothers, the blind, crippled, and the sick, to all of whom the dedicated staff have extended a loving invitation in the name of the Savior. The Mission includes an elementary school, Bible school, Braille school for the blind, adult literacy classes, a public reading room, and a combination of industrial classes where sewing, embroidery, cooking, printing, bookbinding, basket and rope making are taught. Other major institutions are the Krishnabai Memorial Hospital, the Sunset Home for the Aged, the Tuberculosis Sanatorium, and the Dispensary for outpatients. In the center of the compound stands the church.

But most important of all is the loyal and sacrificial staff, consisting of missionaries from many lands and Indians from all parts of the country, in whom the Christ-like spirit of Pandita Ramabai lives on in loving and devoted service.

8

Joseph Hardy Neesima
of Japan

THIS IS THE story of a man who responded to the lure of a foreign land and returned to transform his own. He was the first Japanese Protestant to become prominent in the Christian movement of his country.

Shimeta Neesima was born on February 12, 1843, in Yedo (the present Tokyo), Japan. He was the fifth child but the oldest son of a samurai who was attached to the household of a prince. As one of the minor aristocracy and heir of his branch of the family, he was early given special training in the etiquette befitting his station. His parents and grandparents were Shintoists, deeply religious and faithful in their religious observances. At the age of five he was taken to the temple of the god that was to be his life protector. Writing in later years about his early religious practices, Neesima testified:

I was obedient to my parents, and as they early taught me to do, I served gods made by hand with great reverence. I strictly observed the days of my ancestors and departed friends, and we went to the graveyards to worship their spirits. I often rose up early in the morning, went to a temple which was at least three and a half miles from home, where I worshipped the gods, and returned promptly reaching home before breakfast.[1]

Shimeta was a studious lad with an eager and searching mind. Late at night he would steal away to an empty store-room in a far corner of his grandfather's house, hoping no one would miss him from the bedroom or notice the faint flicker of his crude lantern. There, lying on his stomach on the *tatami* (rush-mat floor), he poured over the Chinese translation of several Western books loaned to him by a friend. He read through a history of the United States and then through a condensed history of the world. Finally one night, he opened a Chinese summary of the Bible, and for the first time in his life was introduced to the Christian faith.

As a flower opens to the sun, so his heart opened to the truth of God's Word. When he read the creation story, he exclaimed with excitement, "It was God who created the world and all things that we see. He created me also. Then I must be grateful to God; I must believe and obey Him!" As a result he began to believe in a Creator-God and felt that his primary allegiance was to him and not to his parents, as his religion taught.

On one occasion Shimeta's grandfather discovered him reading a Chinese translation of *Robinson Crusoe*, a story which completely fascinated the lad. The white-haired grandfather shook his head and said to the boy, "Young man, it does you no good to dabble in such reading. It will fill your head with ideas that may destroy us all."

"But Grandfather," replied Shimeta somewhat impa-

[1] J. D. Davis, *Joseph Hardy Neesima*, p. 43.

tiently, "must we stay shut up like crickets in a bamboo cage; like rats in a sack?" [2]

Neesima soon acquired a knowledge of the Chinese classics and was chosen by his prince to be one of three attendants to study Dutch, the only European language accessible to the Japanese at that time. When he entered his seventeenth year, he was appointed to teach the school of which his father had been in charge, and also to do the duty of a scribe.

At that period great events were stirring the life of Japan. Commodore Perry of the United States Navy had sailed into Yedo Bay in March, 1854, and opened up the two ports of Shimoda and Hakodate to American trade. Not long afterward the first commercial treaties were negotiated between Japan and several foreign powers. The revolution which was soon to alter so profoundly the life of the country had begun. Japan was emerging from its self-imposed isolation from the Western world and was adopting almost feverishly whatever seemed of value of Western Civilization.

Neesima soon became restless. The sight of a Dutch ship in the harbor convinced him of the advanced technology of the Western nations and of the urgent need for industrialization in his own native land. From his reading he developed a great admiration for the United States, especially for its stand on human liberty, and he longed to go to that country for further study. In addition, the new sense of emancipation brought to him by his belief in God led him to take steps to seek escape from the service of his prince and make his way out of Japan.

Finally, young Shimeta managed to persuade his prince to order him off by sea to study in Hakodate, several hundred miles to the north. This was in 1864, when he was twenty-one years of age. In Hakodate he obtained service with Nic-

[2] Marianna and Norman Prichard, *Ten Against the Storm*, p. 13.

olai, a very remarkable missionary, chaplain of the Russian Consulate and founder of the Russian Orthodox Church in Japan. Shimeta became Nicolai's teacher of Japanese, while at the same time he was laboriously learning English from a Japanese clerk of an English shipping firm. It was this friendly clerk who gave Neesima his chance.

He told him of an American schooner about to sail for Shanghai and helped him get in touch with the captain. The kindhearted American captain finally agreed to let Shimeta smuggle himself on board as a stowaway, so that the Japanese officials could not blame the skipper for Neesima's escape. For in those days the law of the land made going abroad a criminal offense.

Under cover of darkness the helpful clerk rowed Neesima out to the schooner as he lay hidden in the bottom of a sampan. He nimbly scrambled over the side of the vessel and hurried below deck, where the captain hid him in a storage closet. For several hours he lay locked up while Japanese customs officers searched the vessel for stowaways. Finally the officials left, and the schooner set sail for Shanghai, carrying a nervous young tramp who had nothing to depend upon except the providence of God.

In Shanghai Neesima cut his hair short and sold his two precious swords, all signs of his knighthood in Japan. He sold his long samurai sword for ocean passage and the short suicide blade to buy a Chinese New Testament. Then he persuaded the captain of another American ship to take him to the United States.

Captain Taylor accepted him as a cabin boy, treated him with considerable kindness, and on the long voyage taught him English and navigation. During his spare time Shimeta pored over the words of the New Testament, and his heart leaped when he came to the wonderful words of John 3:16.

Months later, just after the close of America's Civil War,

the good ship *Wild Rover* brought Shimeta Neesima into Boston Harbor. On the way over he had acquired the nickname "Joe" from the sailors, so he dropped his name Shimeta and took on the biblical name Joseph. It was a fitting symbol, for he had left the old life behind and was now entering the new.

Fortunately, Alpheus Hardy, owner of the *Wild Rover*, was a fine Christian layman. When he heard of Neesima, he took the youth into his home as a servant; but soon recognizing his superior qualities he sent him to Phillips Academy at Andover. It was during his stay there that Joseph was baptized, united with the Seminary Church, and persuaded to return to Japan as a Christian missionary. In his own words he later wrote of this experience:

I date my conversion some time after arrival [in America]; but I was seeking God and His light from the hour I read His Word. With my new experience was born a desire to preach the Gospel among my people. The motive in offering myself to this work is my sympathy with the need of my country, and love for perishing souls; and above all the love of Christ has constrained me to this work.[3]

With such a burden thrust upon him, Joseph entered Amherst College in Massachusetts, graduated in 1870 with a B.S. degree, and then returned to Andover to attend the Theological Seminary. All during this time he was supported by Mr. Alpheus Hardy, so in gratitude he took the surname of his generous benefactor as his middle name.

Mr. Hardy as a young man had desired to enter the ministry, but, prevented by ill health, he went into business, regarded that as a divine calling and resolved to administer for God any money that he should make. Now he felt he was

[3] *Ibid.,* p. 41.

fulfilling a lifelong ambition by preparing someone else to go out and minister to the needy world. Joseph Hardy Neesima, grateful for this God-given opportunity, worked very earnestly and excelled as a student.

He interrupted his seminary course to serve as interpreter to certain Japanese officials of a special embassy which had been sent to study the educational system of the West. For eighteen months he accompanied the embassy as they traveled throughout the United States and Europe. His written report had a marked influence upon the embassy's findings and so helped to mold the new educational structure of Japan.

By the end of the tour, both by his Christian witness and his intellectual ability Joseph had won so deep a respect of the emperor's ministers that they begged him to return to Japan with them for government service. Joseph, however, had his own calling to fulfill and returned to the seminary to finish his training and receive ordination as a minister of the gospel of Jesus Christ.

During his studies in the United States, Joseph Neesima had been gradually formulating a method for reaching Japan with the Christian faith. He came to the conclusion that this could best be accomplished by winning the members of his own class, the samurai, for they were leaders of the nation. If they became Christians, he reasoned, the nation would follow; and the best way to reach them would be through Christian schools such as he had attended. He decided, therefore, to establish for them a Christian institution of higher learning.

At the outset Neesima found little encouragement for his ambitious scheme. The leaders of Japan urged him again and again to accept office in the government and throw in his lot with them. The secretaries of the American Board of Commissioners for Foreign Missions hesitated because of the heavy financial burden involved in the scheme. His own benefactor, Mr. Alpheus Hardy, was dubious of the whole project.

In spite of all the opposition, Neesima steadfastly believed that his plan was of God. At the annual meeting of the American Board in 1874, he presented his purpose with great emotion and determination and cried out to the assembly, "I will not get down from this platform until you promise to help me build this school that my country so desperately needs." The audience was deeply moved and in a few minutes subscribed nearly five thousand dollars for the project.

In December, 1874, Joseph Neesima stood again on Japanese soil after an absence of nearly ten years. He left a stowaway; he returned a missionary. He began his work among the members of his own household and within a short time persuaded them to put their trust in God as revealed in the person of Jesus Christ.

He preached in several towns where he found the people singularly eager to learn about the Christian faith. Very soon Christian churches came into being in the province of his ancestors, near the very heart of Japan.

At the same time Neesima took steps toward the establishment of the school on which he had set his heart. Osaka was his first choice as a site, but a number of difficulties caused him to turn to Kyoto, the ancient capital and cultural center of Japan, a stronghold of Buddhism and Shintoism. At that time there were three thousand five hundred temples and eight thousand priests in the city.

There the young dreamer gained three wonderful friends to help him with his seemingly impossible scheme. One was an American Board missionary from Illinois, a tall Civil War colonel named Jerome Davis, for whom Neesima had gained permission from the government to reside in Kyoto. The second friend was a blind scholar named Kakuma Yamamoto, an adviser to the governing council of the Kyoto area. It was he who helped procure five and a half acres of land for the new school, not far from the grounds of the imperial palace. The third friend was Yamamoto's pretty, quick-witted sister, O-Yae, who not long afterward became Neesima's wife. Their marriage on January 2, 1876, was significant, since it was the first Christian marriage in the city. O-Yae proved to be an understanding companion and entered with great enthusiasm into her husband's dreams and work.

In late November, 1875, with seven dormitory students and one day-scholar, and with Jerome Davis as the only other teacher, Joseph Neesima opened his one-room school, to which he gave the name Doshisha, meaning "the one purpose company." They were not permitted to include the Bible in the course of study, but the governor said that Christianity could be taught under the title of moral science, and that preaching could be done in the homes of the faculty members.

From the very outset the new thirty-two-year-old principal was faced with relentless opposition. The temple priests of the city sought to move heaven and earth to thwart his plans. Viscount Tanaka, influential government official, came down from Tokyo to beg him to abandon his school and accept a key government position. The Viscount was shocked when the young idealist refused.

"Well, Neesima," he remarked, "I see you are indeed a slave of Jesus Christ."

But God was with his faithful servant. Within a few months, two other missionaries arrived from America to join the faculty, and in the following year the first three buildings, one of them a chapel, were completed. Neesima's dream was at last becoming a reality.

That same year the enrollment was suddenly increased by thirty when a group of young men, all samurai, came from the southern island of Kyushu to enter the school. The story behind this influx is in itself amazing.

In 1872, Captain L. L. Janes, an American army officer from West Point, was engaged by a feudal prince of Kyushu to found a military school in the interior city of Kumamoto. Although not a missionary, Captain Janes was a dedicated Christian, filled with a strong desire to win for Christ the nearly hundred young men who were placed under his care. His wife was a daughter of the well-known Dr. Scudder, early medical missionary to India, and she supported her husband's efforts with prayer.

Proceeding cautiously at first, Captain Janes later organized a Bible study group in his home, as a result of which several of the youths were genuinely converted and began to witness among their fellows. A revival swept through the school, and more than half the students made a public decision for Christ.

The climax came when on a Sunday in January, 1876, forty students climbed to the summit of a neighboring hill and covenanted together, signing the document with their blood, to stand by their new faith and to preach the gospel throughout Japan. The action met with loud protest and strong opposition, mostly from the families and friends of the converts. Bitter persecution followed, fathers threatening their sons with the death penalty, mothers threatening to commit suicide in order to atone for what was regarded as degrading to the family name. Some of the boys were imprisoned and others banished from their homes, while a plot was laid, fortunately without success, to kill the whole company.

Captain Janes himself was dismissed from the school, but not before he had providentially learned that a Christian school had recently been opened by Joseph Neesima in Kyoto. Thereupon thirty members of the Kumamoto Band made their way five hundred miles overland to Kyoto and

enrolled in the new Doshisha School. They were a young
and restless lot, none of them as much as twenty years of
age, but from them were to come some of the outstanding
leaders in the Christian movement of Japan.

Neesima immediately planned a course of study for the
young preachers-in-the-making, and they spent three full
years in theological training. Some remained as teachers
and attracted other students from the southern island of
Kyushu.

With the growth of the school, Neesima's burdens mounted
rapidly. He had full charge of the school, and to him came
for settlement all the problems of students and teachers.
Misunderstandings with the American Board on matters of
policy, criticism by non-Christians and Christians including
missionaries, were part of his heavy load. Often he had to
mediate between missionaries and Japanese Christians.

The opening of the Girls' School and a Nurses' Training
School, with the added task of raising an endowment large
enough to put the whole institution on a safe financial
basis, all combined to add to Neesima's mounting responsibility. In addition, he was closely connected with the newly
organized Japanese Home Missionary Society and undertook to conduct preaching missions on its behalf.

Increasingly Neesima became convinced that the Doshisha
must become a university. Up until this time it had been
simply a Christian school with emphasis upon theological
training. The new Government schools were gaining in prestige and attracting many of the better qualified students by
their wide range of courses. In these, religious influence was
negative, the atmosphere being distinctly secular and at
times anti-Christian.

Neesima was convinced that Japan must have a strong
Christian university "to raise up Christian ministers, Christian physicians, Christian statesmen, and even Christian

merchants." "Christians," he argued, "must not be charged with being ignoramuses, or they would not win the respect of the people."

In 1884, Neesima and a Japanese colleague issued an appeal for a university "which is founded upon pure morality and which teaches modern advanced science." They based it on the contention that "all Oriental states are almost destitute of liberty and Christian morality; they cannot . . . rapidly advance in civilization." [4]

Always frail in health, Neesima felt the physical strain of his manifold burdens, so that on the advice of his friends he went to Europe and later to America for rest and recuperation. For a while he became worse and was forced to spend some months in a sanatorium. As his strength began to come back, his vision leaped forward for his beloved Japan. He longed to win all Japan to the Christian faith. He made plans to assist a Christian newspaper in Tokyo and to found a medical school in connection with the Doshisha. He raised money for buildings and equipment and made arrangements for some of his staff to study in America. "Give us money to make the Doshisha into a university!" he pleaded. "We must turn out Christian leaders for a new Christian Japan."

When Neesima returned to Japan late in 1885, he found things Western, including Christianity, riding on the crest of a wave of popularity. Japanese were eager to be accepted by the West and were feverishly adopting whatever came to them from the Occident. Opposition to Christianity, though still vocal, had greatly diminished. Between 1882 and the close of 1888, the membership of Protestant churches increased more than fivefold, and some were even predicting that by the twentieth century Japan would be predominantly Christian.

[4] Kenneth Scott Latourette, *These Sought a Country*, pp. 123-24.

Neesima was given an enthusiastic welcome upon his arrival in Kyoto. The next day, in celebration of the tenth anniversary of the founding of the Doshisha, he laid the cornerstones of two new buildings, and the anniversary exercises were attended by the governor of the province. The Doshisha had become popular, and its president had the respect of high and low. Its graduates were prominent in public affairs.

The nation's most influential men made substantial pledges to implement Neesima's dream of a university. Friends in America also sent their gifts. In Sendai, in the north of Japan, another school was founded under Neesima's supervision, which it was hoped might become a second Doshisha.

Neesima had always been frail. Even during his rest in America he had never fully regained his health, and now under many burdens his strength ebbed. He retired to a small seaside hotel in Oiso to rest, and somehow he knew that death was imminent. His mind set itself to work feverishly through the precious minutes left. Hardly stopping for breath, he dictated to the university officers letters full of his longing to keep the Doshisha true to its Christian course. He was concerned about how much the students and teachers would be willing to sacrifice when Kyoto clamored that their Christian sign must be taken down. "The Doshisha must remain strong," Neesima murmured.

Paul Kanamori, Doshisha's acting president, leaned over to reassure him. "*Sensei* [teacher], please go in peace. We will do everything in our power to carry on your work."

Neesima turned to Pastor Hiromichi Kozaki, who now came to his side. "The third chapter of Ephesians," he whispered. "Will you read it please." Neesima moved his lips as he listened, "that ye, being rooted and grounded in love, may be able to comprehend . . ." [5]

[5] Marianna and Norman Prichard, *Ten Against the Storm*, p. 24.

At twenty minutes past two on the twenty-third of January, 1890, in that bare little room, they heard their beloved president whisper, "Peace, joy, heaven!"

The funeral services took place in Kyoto in the presence of the students, graduates from all parts of the country, provincial and city authorities, and representatives of foreign missions. A large tent had been erected in the college grounds, as the chapel could not accommodate the assembled crowd which numbered over four thousand. Tributes poured in from many government officials and friends; the newspapers were lavish in their praise.

When death overtook this great man of God in the midst of his labors, the Doshisha had grown into an influential and well-equipped institution of nearly nine hundred students. By the end of the first twenty-five years of its existence, 4,611 students had entered the school, while 936 had graduated. Of these graduates, 147 were engaged in teaching, 95 were preaching the gospel, 78 were trained nurses, and over 200 were in various departments of business. By 1955, the eightieth anniversary of the founding, the Doshisha had grown into a university of 23,000 students. Today it is numbered among the leading universities of Japan.

Neesima's dream of the conversion of all Japan has not been realized. Indeed, the percentage of Christians in that land is still less than one percent. The Doshisha which he founded has not always been true to the principles which gave it birth. Yet Neesima's life can by no means be regarded as a failure. In the words of Dr. Kenneth Scott Latourette, leading church historian:

Christians are a small minority in Japan, but they are a growing minority and of their existence and their health Neesima was in part the source. It has been of incalculable value to Protestant Christianity in Japan that at its very beginnings the outstanding indigenous Christian was one of the vision, the transparent unselfishness and devotion, the trained intelligence, and the radiant faith of Neesima. He has been a legacy which can never be fully appraised but for which for untold generations to come Japan will be richer.[6]

[6] Kenneth Scott Latourette, *These Sought a Country*, p. 130.

V
Reformers

"Righteousness exalteth a nation." PROVERBS 14:34

THE AFRO-ASIAN Churches may be compared to small islands in a vast ocean. The Christians are small minorities set amidst huge non-Christian populations. But their influence upon the total life of the nation has been far out of proportion to their numerical strength. Acting like leaven in the dough, they have permeated society with Christian principles, affecting the social, economic, and moral life of the people.

Some leaders of the Afro-Asian Churches have been especially used by God to bring about reforms within society. Chief Khama of Bechuanaland in Southern Africa (now called Botswana), by virtue of his strategic position had the unusual opportunity to raise the moral and economic standards of his entire tribe. Toyohiko Kagawa of Japan had the rare capacity of combining social concern with evangelistic passion, so that he not only touched the lives of individuals but made an impact upon the total life of the nation. Both men came into the Church from without and then went back into the outside world to help transform it.

9

Chief Khama
of Bechuanaland

Kʜᴀᴍᴀ, ᴡʜᴏsᴇ ɴᴀᴍᴇ means antelope, was born in Shoshong, Bechuanaland, sometime around the year 1830. He was the oldest son of Chief Sekhome, ruler of the Bamangwato tribe and a noted witch doctor. Khama could outrun any of his companions and early in his youth was given the name of the antelope that gallops across the veld.

One day, when Khama was a lad of fourteen, men came running into town with the news that a strange man, whose face was white and whose body was covered with cloth, was walking in the direction of their homes. Never before had such a man been seen in their tribe. Excited indeed was the chattering that arose in the mud huts with their circular thatched roofs.

Young Khama walked swiftly at the side of his father-chief along the southward trail to meet the white stranger. He gazed in wonder as he saw a sturdy man, wearing clothes such as he had not seen before and carrying two small boxes under his arm. As he looked into the bronzed face of the traveler, he saw that his eyes and mouth were kind. Khama soon learned that he was a messenger of the Most High God and that his name was David Livingstone.

That evening the lad learned what was in those two boxes. One was a black lacquered container with medicines to make boys and men better when they were ill. The other held a strange object which seemed to open, yet was full of hundreds and hundreds of leaves. He was wonder-struck when the missionary explained to him that the book could speak without making a sound, and that it told about the one, infinite, holy, loving God, who is Father of all men, and whose Son, Jesus Christ, came to teach men to love God and to love one another.

Soon Livingstone left the village; but young Khama never forgot him, and in time other white men came, among them Robert Moffatt, and taught him more about the same book and the same God. Some time later Khama went to stay with Chief Sechele of the neighboring Bakwena tribe, Livingstone's convert and friend, a man of ability and energy who was struggling for the uplift of his hard-pressed people. Here Khama witnessed what Christianity could do for chief and people. From the missionaries he learned how to read and write and began to study the Bible.

On his return home he persuaded his father to invite Christian missionaries to their tribe also. If other chiefs had them, he argued, why not Sekhome? Consequently, in 1858, a German missionary came to Shoshong, the Bamangwato capital, and Khama along with Khamane, his brother, and others were instructed in the Christian faith and baptized. Subsequently Shoshong became a center for the London Missionary Society, and such men as John Mackenzie, John Smith Moffat, J. D. Hepburn, and W. C. Willoughby came and preached the gospel to the people of Bamangwato.

At the time of his baptism Khama was just over thirty
years of age, a splendid specimen of manhood. "He was well
over six feet in height, with a frame like whipcord, the swift-
est runner, the surest hunter, and the finest rider in the tribe,
full of dignity in his bearing, yet gentle and winsome as a
child." [1]

On one occasion, with a group of picked hunters from the
tribe, Khama set out on the spoor of a great lion that had
made itself the terror of the countryside. Night after night
the lion had leaped among their oxen and had slain the
choicest in the chief's herd. Again and again the hunters
had gone out on his trail; but always they returned empty-
handed, though boasting loudly of what they would do if
they ever found the animal.

That night, as the men sat around the fire, each one
bragged how he would slay the lion the next day and thus
become the hero of the tribe. Khama listened in silence,
scarcely able to restrain his contempt for those who swag-
gered so much and did so little. After the hunters had rolled
themselves in their animal skins and were fast asleep around
the camp fire, he slung his gun over his shoulder and slipped
out into the starry night.

The night passed. As the first flush of dawn pierced the
horizon and the men began to roll out of their animal skins,
they gazed in awed amazement. For they saw, striding toward
them, their tall young prince; and over his shoulders hung
the tawny skin and mane of a full-grown king lion. Alone in
the night he had slain the terror of the tribe!

When Khama became a Christian, he dedicated all his
valor and prowess to the service of his Master. His allegiance
to Christ and to Christian principles was an example to all.
He chose a fine Christian girl to be his wife, whom he affec-

[1] G. A. Gollock, *Sons of Africa*, p. 93.

tionately called Ma-Bessie, and together they built a Christian home full of refinement and love. Their home was a model of cleanliness, order, and discipline.

The Christian concept of marriage strongly appealed to Khama. When his father insisted that he, as the son of a great chief, must marry other wives to uphold his status, he firmly refused. He was willing, he said, to meet any test of obedience his father might set, but Ma-Bessie was his one true wife, and he would not go against the law of God.

Khama also took a strong stand against the pagan practices of his tribe. He had nothing to do with traditional ceremonies by which the boys were initiated into full tribal status. He felt that several of the customs connected with these initiation rites were immoral and, to say the least, harmful. He discounted all claims of sorcery and rain-making incantations. He was particularly staunch in his denunciation of strong drink. In every respect Khama was a sincere and intelligent Christian.

Khama's insistence on Christian principles soon aroused the indignation of his father, who still persisted in his paganism. There began a series of threats and attacks, and for several years the life of the young prince was in constant danger.

One night Sekhome posted armed soldiers around the hut of his son and ordered them to open fire. The men, however, refused to obey, for Khama was their idol. The chief, expecting vengeance, fled, but Khama sent him a message of forgiveness.

On another night Sekhome set a group of sorcerers to work against his son. Khama was awakened by the sound of strange clashing and chanting, and looking out he saw the wizards dancing with horns and lions' teeth clanking about their necks and with manes of animal hair waving above their painted faces. As they danced they cast charms into the fire and chanted weird spells on Khama. The young Christian never hesitated. He strode forward swiftly, scattered the witch doctors and stamped out the fire.

Under a hundred insults and threats Khama stood silent, never once seeking revenge and always treating his treacherous father with respect.

Macheng, Khama's uncle, who had long been in banishment, now appeared on the scene. In a foolish moment Sekhome, possibly out of sheer desperation, had offered him the chieftainship if he would kill Khama and Khamane. Macheng was glad to become the chief, but to Sekhome's dismay he refused to slay his nephews and rather tended to treat them with favor. Sekhome then sought to reinstate himself as chief, but Macheng made short work of his maneuvers and banished him from the tribe. Before long, however, Macheng found that the ways of his two Christian nephews were a rebuke to himself, so he turned against the two young men. First he tried charms and sorcery, then poison. Things went from bad to worse. The people proposed that Macheng be banished and Sekhome be recalled, but now the latter refused to return.

At last Khama, seeing that his tribe was headed for ruin, appealed for help to Chief Sechele, his ever faithful friend. Sechele dispatched his oldest son with a band of warriors who quickly expelled Macheng and would have shot him had not Khama intervened. Macheng went into exile and ultimately drank himself to death. In the fall of 1872, Khama became chief of the Bamangwato by the election of the headmen.

His Christian faith was soon put to test. It was September, the season when the people began to dig their gardens. This was always preceded by certain pagan ceremonies. After consultation with two missionaries, Chief Khama assembled his people in the public courtyard on Sunday morning. In a short but pointed speech, he emphatically announced his unwavering determination to adhere to Christian principles. He did not prohibit their usual ceremonies; but they must not be performed in the *kotla* (the chief's open-air enclosure for official meetings) and, as chief, he would contribute nothing toward them. Whoever wished to have his seed or garden charmed, could do so at his own expense; but he himself would follow no such custom. The missionaries were then requested to conduct a brief service, asking God to bless their gardens and their efforts, after which the people were told they might start digging whenever they pleased.

Affairs did not go smoothly with the new chief. He refused to "make rain" with pagan ceremonies, and his brother Khamane, having partly relapsed into paganism, became hostile to him. Early in 1873, against the judgment of his friend Sechele, Khama recalled his father to Shoshong, probably from filial feelings. But the inveterate old chief soon reverted to his old habit of plotting and began to stir up strife. Khama, with great prudence, withdrew from Shoshong to Serowe, a cattle post about forty miles to the north. So great was his personal influence that the majority of the young men of the tribe followed him, leaving behind five thousand empty huts in the capital. Sekhome carried on miserably for a couple of years, and finally, as the situation deteriorated, Khama returned to Shoshong and once again assumed rulership over the tribe. His father fled into exile.

Khama immediately turned his attention to establishing order throughout the land. For the next ten years his work was uphill and difficult, but slowly and steadily he accomplished his beneficent will in Shoshong. Under the power of the gospel, with wise and tactful leadership, he made it one of the model towns in South Africa. No compulsion was used. Unlike the Bakwena chief Sechele, who in his early days with Livingstone wanted to make his people Christians by the use of his hippopotamus whip, Khama knew that any changes worth having must begin in the heart.

In the course of time, all religious functions in the *kotla* at Shoshong became Christian. Khama himself conducted two services there every Sunday, standing beneath the ancient tree of justice with the open sky overhead. Later he erected a large stone church in the center of town. The customary pagan rites at harvest time were displaced by Christian prayer and thanksgiving.

Law and order were established throughout the land. By his courage and genius Khama was able to repel the chief of the Matabele who had struck fear into the Bamangwato for many years. Thieving ceased so completely that travelers set no night watch on their wagons when they camped on Khama's ground. He issued a decree against the purchase of slaves and abolished the customary *bogadi* or purchase of wives by cattle. He introduced a law of marriage from free choice, at an age when young men and women were capable of making an intelligent selection.

Chief Khama's attitude toward the Marsawa or bushmen who lived within his boundaries is an illustration of his genuine Christian spirit. No other African ruler cared for these despised and downtrodden desert dwellers as did he. Even the Christians at first called them "dogs without souls." Khama treated them with respect and spoke of them kindly as "my people." He punished those who treated them cruelly; he even tried to evoke their self-respect by showing confidence in them. A bushman who formerly spoke of himself as "your dog" was heard to say one day, "I, I am a person."

Missionaries and travelers alike bore witness to Chief Khama's high qualities of leadership. Mr. J. D. Hepburn, one of the British missionaries stationed at Shoshong, described his work and influence in these words:

Out of the ruins of anarchy, lawlessness, and general disorder, he has been building up law, order, and stability. His people are living in peace, his fields are laden with corn, the white man's home is as sacred as in his own country, and a purer morality is growing up from day to day.[2]

A traveler who spent a week in Shoshong wrote about its chief:

Khama has established peace, prosperity, and justice in all his borders. His word is law. He pervades everything in his town. He is always on horseback visiting the fields, the stores, and the outlying kraals. He has a word for everyone: he calls every woman "my daughter" and every man "my son," he pats the little children on the head. He is a veritable father of his people.[3]

Khama and the missionaries were on excellent terms, working in close cooperation for the welfare of the tribe. He gave full support to their activities, while he always sought their advice in matters of religion. Through his influence many Bamangwato people became Christians, and the work of the London Missionary Society flourished.

The intimacy that prevailed between Khama and the missionaries was like that which exists between men of a common racial heritage. In particular, Khama's ideals of Christian womanhood and the purity of his own home life made it possible for him to enter into the fellowship of the missionaries' family lives. On many occasions, when the husbands were absent on extended evangelistic tours, their wives and children were left under Khama's sole protection and guardianship. No brother could have cared for them with greater thoughtfulness and kindness.

But things, of course, were not always smooth. At times,

[2] J. D. Hepburn, *Twenty Years in Khama's Country*, p. 122.
[3] J. T. Bent, *The Ruined Cities of Mashohaland*, p. 27.

Khama could be very autocratic and stubborn; once his
confidence was lost, it was not easy to regain it. After many
years of close fellowship the chief and Mr. Hepburn had a
serious misunderstanding, which was healed only after many
attempts at reconciliation by the other missionaries.

Chief Khama's greatest moral battle was against the curse
of drunkenness that prevailed among his people. One particular experience in his youth had turned him into a determined
prohibitionist. His father, on one occasion, went to see a
white trader about the purchase of a horse that had caught
his eye. Young Khama accompanied him, taking along five
excellent tusks of ivory as barter for the horse. The trader
was an unscrupulous man who sought to take advantage of
the chief. Khama saw with dismay that he was giving more
and more brandy to his father. At last the trader tried to
induce the chief to part with the tusks of ivory for two bars
of lead and a small amount of gunpowder. Sekhome ordinarily
never permitted his sons to interfere with him, and he was
a dangerous man when his temper was roused. But Khama
could not stand by and see his father cheated and dishonored
in this fashion. As the old man became more and more incapable of reasoning, Khama suddenly ordered the servants
to pick up the intoxicated chief and carry him and the ivory
back home. He well knew the punishment that awaited him
next morning. But as he walked home behind the servants
and their miserable burden, he determined in his heart that
he would henceforth fight drink as long as he lived.

Shortly after his inauguration as chief, Khama enacted
a law against the importation and sale of alcohol in his
kingdom, but there were those who constantly opposed his
legislation.

On one occasion, when Khama was engaged in repelling an
attack by the harassing Matabele, he left his younger brother,
Khamane, in charge of affairs in Shoshong. When he rode

back into town, he discovered to his dismay a group of men and women in the midst of a drunken spree. His own brother was the ringleader. For once Khama lost his temper. He seized a burning torch and, running to the hut of Khamane, set fire to the roof and burned the house down over his drunken brother's head. He ordered all the beer that had been brewed to be seized and poured out upon the veld. The old men of the tribe muttered against him and threatened to kill him. Khama met them face to face.

"When I was still a lad," he thundered, "I used to think how I would govern my town and what kind of a kingdom it should be. One thing I determined, I would not rule over a drunken town or people. I will not have drink in this town. If you must have it, you must go."

The worst defaulters, however, were not Africans themselves but the white traders who smuggled their liquor into the land. One night a group of these men met together in one of the homes and had a wild party. Drinking led to fighting, there was a noisy brawl, and Khama himself was called to the spot where he witnessed the disgraceful orgy.

Two days later the traders were summoned before him. His stern words cut like a whip. "I am trying," he said, "to lead my people to act according to the Word of God which we have received from you white people, and yet *you* show them an example of wickedness such as we never knew. You," and his voice rose in burning scorn, "you, the people of the Word of God! I make an end of this curse today. Go! Take your cattle and possessions and leave my town and never come back again!"

For a while no man moved or spoke. Then one of the traders who had lived in the town since he was a lad pleaded with Khama for pity as an old friend.

"You, 'my friend'?" said the chief with biting irony, "you, the ringleader of those who despise my laws? You are my worst enemy. You pray for pity? No, for you I have no pity. It is my duty to have pity on my people over whom God has placed me, and I am going to show them pity today; that is my duty to them and to God. . . . Go!" [4]

Perhaps the greatest contribution Chief Khama made to his people was his fight to save their land from the selfish foreigner. Other chiefs, tempted by one lure or another, granted freehold rights to the white settlers, but Khama never parted with an acre of his tribal lands. When Cecil Rhodes of South Africa aspired to absorb Khama's country and other neighboring regions in the sphere of the British East Africa Company, Khama resisted with all his might. He and two other African chiefs visited England under missionary escort in 1895 and put their case before the British Government. They argued with such sincerity and persuasion that the Secretary of State for the Colonies gave his decision in their favor.

Even though he accepted the formal establishment of the British Protectorate in 1885, he laid down conditions reserving not only the ownership of land, but the right to decide all cases arising among his people by customary law, and to maintain existing legislation against the liquor traffic.

Chief Khama celebrated the golden jubilee of his reign in the summer of 1922. Congratulations were heaped upon him as government officials, missionaries, and tribesmen in a great assembly bore testimony to the high quality of his leadership. Khama himself, hale and full of vigor, made a great speech in which he recounted the blessings which the Christian faith had brought, expressed his gratitude to the white men who were his friends, and closed with an impassioned appeal to his people to depart from all pagan practices and wholeheartedly serve the true God of Heaven.

[4] Basil Mathews, *The Book of Missionary Heroes,* pp. 146-47.

Less than a year later, in February, 1923, Khama's long life came to an end. Caught in a rainstorm while out riding, he took a severe chill and, after a brief illness, died peacefully, surrounded by his friends. He was over ninety years of age.

The news was cabled to all parts of the world. The headlines read: "Oldest king in the world dies; great African reformer made Bechuanaland the first modern prohibition country."

The monument erected to his memory, unveiled with full honors by the Prince of Wales in 1925, bears an inscription on its base, "Righteousness exalteth a nation," a fitting memorial for a man who by precept and example turned a whole savage tribe into a peaceful and industrious Christian people. As one witness put it, "To pass from Bechuanaland before Khama to Bechuanaland after Khama was like passing from Dante's Inferno to his Paradise."

10

Toyohiko Kagawa
of Japan

Toyohiko Kagawa was born on July 10, 1888, in the "Year of the Rat," the twenty-first year of the Emperor Meiji's reign. The wise old women who attended his birth declared it was an auspicious time to be born, for the rat symbolized plenty. As the rat found plenty of grain, they said, so the child would find riches, honor, and prosperity in his lifetime.

Toyohiko's father was a wealthy and important nobleman, called Denjiro Kagawa, the owner of one of Kobe's principal shipping companies. He was also Secretary to the Privy Council and as such had the standing of a minister in the emperor's cabinet. He and his wife, Michi, had lived in a large farmhouse at Awa, on the island of Shikoku across the bay from Kobe.

Denjiro Kagawa was a man of hard-driving energy and considerable business acumen, but he was at the same time sensual, wanton, and unprincipled. Early in his married life

142

he left his legal wife to care for the farm at Awa and went to live with a geisha in Kobe, whose name was Kame. Five children were born out of this relationship, the third being Toyohiko. Toyohiko always remembered his mother, Kame, as the gentlest and most beautiful woman he had known. If he gained some of his energy and ingenuity from his father, there is little doubt that he inherited his gentle, sensitive nature from his mother, and that it was transformed by a deep Christian experience into profound compassion for all men.

When Toyohiko was just a lad of four, tragedy suddenly swept over the Kagawa household. Denjiro, the father, largely as the result of his self-indulgence and dissipation, became ill and died. Two months later, Kame fell ill and died as suddenly as her husband had done. The spacious Kobe house was sold and its furniture disposed of. Little Toyohiko and his sister, Ei, were sent to the farmhouse at Awa to live with their father's legal wife and her ill-tempered mother. Loneliness and a morbid sense of insecurity suddenly began to haunt them.

It was to be expected that Toyohiko and Ei would be unwelcome in the Awa household. To Michi Kagawa they represented all the years of infidelity and unhappiness that had followed her marriage to Denjiro. For twenty-five years she and her mother had slaved to manage the farm and had put up with a meager existence, while Denjiro had lived in wealth and in sensual delight. Unconsciously they began to heap all the resentment and bitterness of the years upon the young lad and his sister. Toyohiko, accustomed to comfort and affection, was thrust suddenly into a world where he was bullied, half-starved, and made to work like a little slave. He felt unloved and unwanted, and to a sensitive child with Toyohiko's early upbringing this was almost unbearable. At times the young lad wished that, like his mother, he too could die.

This sense of loneliness and isolation drove Toyohiko to seek comfort in the world of nature and, a little later, in books. During his spare time he roamed the countryside on his own, exalting in the beauties of nature and meditating on the meaning of life. After he learned in school how to read, he began to spend more and more of his time poring over the old scrolls and books which he discovered in the family treasure-room. Toyohiko was a naturally quick and alert child, and as the years passed he moved swiftly to the top of his class. The more he learned, the more he longed for still more learning.

Religion formed the main part of his school curriculum. Young Kagawa learned the Confucian classics with their emphasis on filial piety and patriotism, and he faithfully took part in all the Buddhist ceremonies. It was drilled into his mind that to forsake one's ancestral religion for another was unthinkable to a loyal Japanese.

When he was only ten years old, Toyohiko was admitted into the Middle School across the bay at Tokushima. Here again he found himself in an entirely new world. He found the boys in the dormitory crude, ill-mannered, and unpleasant. The older students boasted freely about their drinking and their sexual adventures. There was a good deal of homosexuality. Toyohiko was revolted and appalled by what he saw. At the same time he was entering a new world of thought, and he plunged into his studies with increased enthusiasm and devotion.

It was soon apparent to the young student that, if he were to achieve anything in the new world, he must learn English. A number of other boys had the same idea, so Toyohiko joined the group of eager students who went to the homes of Dr. Harry Myers, an American Presbyterian minister, and his brother-in-law, Dr. Logan, to learn the language which would open the way to success. This was his first contact with Christian missionaries. Toyohiko made rapid progress in his study, and before long he was asking for English books to read. Dr. Myers lent him a New Testament, and he needed no urging to try to read it. He was immediately fascinated by the story of the Man who lived close to nature but loved men, especially the destitute ones, still more than he did the lilies and the birds. The ethical teaching of the gospel made little impression on him, but the character of Jesus caught hold of his mind and heart.

Just about this time, tragedy struck again. Toyohiko's elder brother, Tanichi, had inherited the vast Kagawa fortune and had up until this time been responsible for all his school expenses. Then, quite suddenly, Tanichi died, and it was discovered that he had been far more profligate than his dissolute father. He had squandered the whole family fortune on wine and women. Moreover, he had pledged the family property, even the farmhouse at Awa. All that was left was a one-room storehouse into which the three women, Michi, her mother, and Ei, had to squeeze with their few personal belongings. The school fees stopped. Toyohiko's situation would have been hopeless indeed, had it not been for a rich uncle who came to his rescue and undertook to give him shelter and continue his schooling.

These fresh troubles drove Toyohiko into a new state of despondency. The thought that haunted him most was that he, too, might suffer the same fate as both his father and his elder brother. He lost all faith in man's ability to live a decent life.

In this state of mind Toyohiko one day heard Dr. Myers narrate for the first time the story of the crucifixion. Tears streamed down the face of the young lad. "Is this true?" he asked.

The missionary nodded. "Quite true."

"But why did he have to die, after all the good he had done?" he asked.

"He died because he loved us," came the quiet answer.

Before he left the missionary's study that evening, Toyohiko Kagawa knelt on the mat and made his first Christian prayer. "O God, make me like Christ!" he asked, sincerely. Suddenly the despair was lifted. Toyohiko knew that a new power had come into his life; he would not follow in the footsteps of his father and his brother; he could become like Christ.

In spite of his newfound joy, Kagawa made no profession of his new faith, either at home with his uncle or in school among the students. He was fully aware of the hostile attitude toward Christianity that prevailed among the Japanese of his day.

One day Dr. Myers questioned him directly. "Kagawa, don't you think you should be baptized?"

"No," he replied quickly. "If I did, my family would disown me."

"What then?" asked the missionary.

"Well . . . ," he stammered uncomfortably. "I should be unable to come to school any more."

The missionary looked at him squarely. "So you are a coward?"

Toyohiko was not angry. He knew his teacher spoke the truth. The only answer lay in action. And so at the tender age of fifteen he was baptized a Christian and took his public stand for Christ. To his surprise, his uncle made no serious objection and allowed the new convert to stay on in the household and continue his studies at school.

Not long after, Kagawa met the first real test of his new faith. Japan had recently declared war on Russia and was in the midst of a costly and bloody struggle. Men were conscripted into the army and young boys were drilled in the schools. With the rest of the students Kagawa was led out on to the parade ground for his first drill. But all he could hear in his mind were the words of Jesus, "Love your enemies," and all he could see was Christ dying without resistance on the cross. Suddenly he flung his rifle to the ground.

"Kagawa! Pick up your gun!"

Toyohiko neither moved nor replied. The crowd went tense, while the instructor's face flushed with anger.

"Why don't you obey me?"

In the silence Toyohiko's reply could be heard across the parade ground. "Because I believe Japan is wrong to go to war!"

The next moment he was knocked to the ground and the infuriated instructor kept on kicking him in the face and stomach. When the ordeal was over, he dragged himself to his feet and stumbled from the field.

This was Toyohiko's first stand for pacifism, a stand for which he had to pay a great price all through his life, but from which he never wavered even the slightest, right down to the end. This stand lost him many friends but won for him the respect of the world.

One day young Kagawa accompanied Dr. Myers on one of his regular visits to the filthy slums of Tokushima, where the beggars, thieves, and outcasts of the city lived. There amidst the dirt and degradation he met a most remarkable young man, who in his teens had fled from Osaka to Tokyo to escape the police, was miraculously converted in a gospel-hall in Tokyo, and then had come to live in the slums of Tokushima to serve the degraded and fallen as he felt Christ himself would have done.

This experience had such a profound effect on the thinking of Kagawa that by the time he was seventeen his mind was clear as he looked into the future. His uncle, proud of his nephew's academic progress, urged him to go to the Imperial University in Tokyo and prepare himself for a position of leadership in the business and political world. He offered to meet all expenses. But Toyohiko declined the offer. "No, Sir," he declared. "I have no desire to go to Tokyo. I intend to be a Christian minister."

This was too much for the uncle. Angrily he laid down an ultimatum: Tokyo or out! A day or so later, Toyohiko packed a few clothes and left the Isobe household, disinherited and penniless. Once again he was without security, but this time he had his faith in Christ.

Carrying his small bundle of clothes, Toyohiko made his way to Dr. Myers' house and told him what had happened. After a brief consultation they decided he should enter the Presbyterian College in Tokyo, and that funds must be found to make it possible. So off to the capital he went after all, but with a different motive than that suggested by his ambitious uncle.

Here at the college Kagawa's stand on pacifism got him into trouble again. The war with Russia was still on, and Kagawa took his stand firmly on the side of Christian pacifism against the almost united opposition of the whole college. One evening he was summoned to the athletic field by one of the students. When he arrived, a group of angry young men surged toward him, and, yelling "traitor," they knocked him to the ground and kicked him mercilessly. "This will knock your pacifism out of you!" they shouted and stood aside to jeer his agony. Toyohiko rose slowly to his knees, clasped his trembling hands together, and in a clear voice prayed, "Father, forgive them, for they know not what they do."

One by one, ashamed and speechless, his attackers turned away and slunk off the field.

When his time at the Tokyo College was over, Kagawa moved back to Kobe, where he intended to enroll in a newly opened theological seminary. Meanwhile he became assistant to a pastor in the city and engaged himself in preaching and "open-air work." Day after day he walked across the bridge into the notorious slum Shinkawa—haunt and refuge of criminals, prostitutes, vagabonds, and murderers—and preached the gospel of God's love to anyone who would give him a hearing. Hardly anyone listened. Nobody cared when, at the end of forty days, he collapsed and did not come back to the slum area.

Friends carried him to Shinkawa and put him to bed in the pastor's house. He was suffering from tuberculosis of the lungs, and all hope for his recovery was abandoned. For three days his friends thought he would die, and even Dr. Myers was summoned to be with him in his last hours. Then a miracle occurred. The crisis suddenly passed and the patient began to get better. Once off his bed, he quickly gathered enough strength to go back to his preaching across the river. Again he collapsed, and this time Dr. Myers had him admitted to the hospital. He stayed there for four unhappy, restless months and then set off for the shores of Atzuma Bay, where he lived in a poverty-stricken fishing village for a whole year, in an attempt to regain his health.

Upon his recovery he returned to Kobe and rejoined the ministerial students at the seminary. Immediately he tried to make up for the year he had lost. Fluent in reading English, he turned to German so that he might read the great theologians and philosophers in their own tongue. He also read through the whole series of a Japanese encyclopedia, from cover to cover.

But the call of the destitute and the forlorn in the slums kept haunting him, and soon Kagawa became restless in his studies. He was convinced that if the people of the slums were to be won for Christ, he must go and live among them, sharing their poverty and suffering. One day, his mind made up, he went to see his beloved teacher. "Dr. Myers," he said quietly, "I have changed my mind. I do not wish to be an ordained minister. I am going to live in the slums."

And so on Christmas Day, 1909, Toyohiko Kagawa, a young man of twenty-one, pushed a handcart with his personal belongings across the Higurashi Bridge in Kobe.

Shinkawa was typical of the slum areas which surrounded the great cities of Japan in those days. In eleven main alleyways lived eleven thousand people. Some were underpaid laborers; others were the socially unwanted. There were murderers, pickpockets, gamblers, prostitutes, epileptics, drunkards, ragpickers; and children, children everywhere. The filth and the stench were almost unbearable.

Kagawa's first place of residence was a so-called haunted house, actually a hut, six feet by nine, with walls made of bamboo. The floors were fouled by dogs, and vermin crawled everywhere. A thin partition divided the hut into two tiny rooms. On the first night of his residence Kagawa shared his quarters with a loathsome looking young man, his face and body disfigured with dermatitis. The next night came a man who had once been a bean-curd vendor but had served a term in prison for murder. The third night it was an alcoholic. And so it went, night after night, as the vagrants moved in.

Kagawa soon developed a regular schedule of activity. He rose before dawn, spent some time in meditation, and then went out to wash and collect water at the hydrant. At six o'clock he stood at one of the crossings and preached to all who would listen. The mornings he spent working at college or sweeping chimneys, which brought him about twenty-one yen per month (about $6.00). Some days he would preach again at two o'clock in the afternoon; on others, he spoke in the evening. In between, he talked to any who would listen, or read and wrote in his hut.

Slowly as the weeks went by, Kagawa was accepted by the people of the slum. He became known as "the preacher" and, a little later, as "the Christian."

But at times he suffered severely at the hands of violent men. Once a drunken man tried to stab him as he began preaching. A bully knocked him over, breaking four of his teeth. A gambler tried to set fire to his hut. An angry brothel owner threatened him with a pistol because he preached against prostitution. Each time Kagawa made no attempt to retaliate but demonstrated the love and patience of his Master.

A few months after he moved in, the three houses next door fell vacant. Toyohiko rented them at once, took down the slim dividing walls and turned the houses into one long, narrow hall. Every Sunday and on evenings of the week, he used it for his preaching services and Sunday School. At night he put up temporary screens and turned the hall into a hostel for the homeless and destitute. In time he was able to establish a small dispensary, with the occasional clinical services of a Christian doctor. Help came from the college and the churches as the work expanded. Missionaries and Japanese Christians made occasional gifts of money and even came down to assist with the Sunday School and the distribution of food to the beggars. An unknown American who heard of Toyohiko's work promised to send fifty dollars a month.

All this made heavy demands on Kagawa's time and health. He was still not fully recovered from the tuberculosis which he had previously contracted. More than once he collapsed while preaching in the open air and had to be carried to his home. In addition, he contracted trachoma, a painful eye disease, from a beggar who stayed at his hostel. This greatly distressed him and later robbed him of the sight of one eye.

Meanwhile, romance began to enter the life of Toyohiko

Kagawa. For some time he had been visiting a bookbinding factory, with its forty or so women workers, trying to interest them in the Christian faith. The forewoman, Haru Shiba, took great interest in Kagawa's preaching and work, and in the course of time was baptized as a Christian in his mission hut. The acquaintance soon blossomed into romance, and in May, 1914, the couple was married in the Kobe church by Dr. Harry Myers. For Toyohiko, it was the end of solitariness. For Haru, it was the beginning of a period of unending work and grim poverty. Her first night of marriage was spent in a hut shared by the destitute, and the first meal she cooked next morning was for fourteen people besides herself and her husband. But for both it was the prelude to a life full of service and joy.

A few months after his marriage, Kagawa decided that, if he were to serve Japan as he really hoped, he must take further training in America. Missionaries and friends rallied to his support, and in August, 1914, three days after the outbreak of World War I, Toyohiko set sail for the United States. He enrolled at Princeton University and at the end of two years gained his doctorate in Philosophy along with a good deal of experience in social service in the slums of American cities. Meanwhile, in Japan, his wife Haru attended a concentrated study course and graduated from high school, in order to be of greater assistance to her husband in his work.

Though his stay in the United States was relatively short, it was long enough to give Kagawa a whole new attitude toward his work. Up to the time he left for America, he had been content to preach a gospel of love and to practice it in service to individuals. He had been so busy among poor people that he had not thought about dealing with the cause of poverty itself. Now he was aware that he would have to attack the root of the problem. He had left Shinkawa as a social worker; he returned as a reformer.

Kagawa saw his ministry now taking three distinct directions. He must prove that Christianity was not just a pious exhortation far removed from the actual business of living. It was closely related to life and to people. To demonstrate this he must continue to live in the confining, sordid environment of Shinkawa. But at the same time, he must go out in the name of Christ and attempt to find a solution to the labor problem of Japan.

About this time certain incidents took place which were destined to bring nationwide publicity to Toyohiko Kagawa. Some time previously, in Tokyo, the laborers had organized the Laborers' Benefit Society, a kind of cooperative organization, but now they sought to expand the Society into the Japanese Federation of Labor. Kagawa accepted the challenge to become the founder of the Kobe branch and began to build up its membership among the workers in the shipyards. Soon afterward he was elected National Secretary of the Federation. Officialdom watched the development warily. In 1919 Kagawa published a book called *The Adoration of the Laborer*. He was immediately arrested and charged with seditious intentions. But there was nothing for which the court could hold him, and they had to let him go. The following year he published *Across the Death-Line*, a novel based on life in the slums. The book created a sensation never experienced before in Japanese publishing history. Its first edition was sold out immediately, and printing after printing was required to meet the public demand. For some time it sold at the rate of a hundred thousand copies a year. As an author, Kagawa's fame was suddenly nationwide. More important, the attention of the whole country was directed toward conditions in the slums.

In the middle of 1921, Kagawa was faced with his first great test in the Labor Federation. Thirty thousand dockyard workers in Kobe decided to go on strike and asked

Kagawa to be their leader. He agreed and formed them into a Trade Union on condition that they refrain from violence. News of the strike was sent out all over the country. Kagawa, the famous author from the slums, had defied the government and broken the law. For in those days strikes were illegal in Japan and so were unions.

For days the situation was tense. Kagawa demonstrated his great qualities of leadership by effectively dealing, on the one hand, with policemen and shipowners and, on the other hand, with agitators in his own ranks. Finally the police decided to end the strike by arresting its leader. Kagawa was mercilessly beaten and dragged to the police station. After two weeks, however, he was released and received a tremendous welcome from the waiting strikers.

The following morning Kagawa heard that a large group of laborers was marching to the shipyards, led by Communist agitators with intent to destroy the machinery and ships and damage the cargoes. He ran out ahead of the mob and single-handedly stopped them, persuading them to accept the way of negotiation and peace. Deserting their Communist leaders and cheering Kagawa, the strikers dispersed.

This was enough to convince the shipowners of the sincerity of Kagawa and his followers. Peaceful negotiations followed; the Trade Union was recognized; new conditions of labor were accepted. Toyohiko Kagawa was a name known all over Japan. And he was only thirty-three years of age.

Not long afterward, Kagawa organized the first Agricultural Union of Japan, followed by the first Japan Peasants Union.

On September 1, 1923, the worst natural catastrophe in living memory struck Japan without warning. A sudden severe earthquake, followed by a tidal wave and then by fire, left nearly all of Yokohama and half of Tokyo in ruins. A hundred thousand people lay dead; five million were homeless.

Communications in the two cities almost ceased to exist. Factories and hospitals lay in ruins. Food was gone. There was no proper water supply. Dysentery and cholera threatened the inhabitants.

Kagawa, assisted by his able wife, rushed to the rescue. From Kobe and Osaka he collected large amounts of food, clothes, and bedding. He transported the supplies to Tokyo by sea, and immediately set about establishing relief centers. Very soon mission authorities sent help and workers, Christian friends in Tokyo lent their assistance, and the government watched him at work. When an Imperial Economic Commission was set up by the emperor, Kagawa was invited to join, the only man chosen from the ranks of the people. His vast knowledge and practical experience were a great help in the rehabilitation and rebuilding schemes of the Commission, while his Christian spirit and sincerity made a profound influence upon the members.

Kagawa soon found himself appointed to serve on other Government Commissions—on unemployment, the organization of Labor Exchanges, and emigration. Largely through his influence, an Anti-Exploitation Land Act was enacted, and by 1925, the law against Trade Unions was repealed, making it possible for labor to legally organize itself. His great triumph came in 1926, when a law was passed which put an end to the slums. A six-year plan was initiated, with a budget of eight million dollars, for rehousing the tens of thousands of people who lived in the overcrowded areas of six of the leading cities of Japan.

In 1930, Mayor Horikira of Tokyo invited Kagawa to become Chief of the Welfare Department in the city and offered him an annual salary of six thousand dollars. Kagawa smiled gently. "I can't become an official and take over the chief's job," he said, "for I have too many commitments in the Church just now. But," he continued, "if you wish me to help, I will agree to become Chief Adviser, without salary of any kind, and spend ten days a month in the service of the Welfare Department."

The program he helped carry through was immense. He first secured shelter for the homeless. Then he tackled the problem of the 31,000 boatmen who lived in six-by-nine-foot shacks on Tokyo's two hundred miles of canals, getting them housed and making provision for the education of their children. He carried through the opening of eleven new social settlements in the worst-hit areas of the city. Available work was distributed among the unemployed, while a scheme for unemployment benefit and insurance was also worked out. Gradually, under an administration free from graft and corruption, the depression was met and the situation changed for the better.

Amid all his manifold activities as social worker and reformer, Kagawa never gave up his evangelistic passion. "Unions are necessary," he said, "but labor problems can only be solved by a change in the heart of the laborer himself." He earnestly coveted the people of Japan for Christ. In 1928, he initiated the "Kingdom of God Movement," a daring, nationwide evangelistic campaign to win a million Japanese to Christ. He spent twenty days of each month traveling and preaching from place to place. The central theme of his preaching was the Cross of Christ and the love of God. His own example of compassion and self-denial gave power to his words, so that wherever he preached men listened with rapt attention.

It wasn't long, however, before Kagawa's conviction concerning pacifism involved him in trouble with the Japanese Government.

In September, 1931, when his country made a sudden attack on Manchuria, Kagawa apologized to the people of China on behalf of the Christians in Japan. He simply said, clearly and with tears in his eyes, that Japan's action was wrong. In the "Friends of Jesus" magazine he wrote: "To my brethren in China. Forgive the sin of Japan. Though Japanese Christians have not the power to oppose military force, some of them regret the sin of Japan. I wish the day of reconciliation may soon come."

On July 7, 1937, Japan declared war on China. Kagawa was more deeply stricken than ever before. He wept for China, for Japan, and for the Church. Then in September, 1939, World War II broke out in Europe, and against a background of rising war hysteria Kagawa the pacifist worked on.

It was in August, 1940, when victory seemed almost certain for the Axis powers, that Kagawa was arrested for the first time as a traitor. As he preached a vigorous sermon on nonviolence one Sunday morning, he noticed two sullen-looking men sitting toward the back of the church. As soon as the sermon was ended, the men moved forward and hustled the preacher out through the silent congregation. But Kagawa was not without friends in high places. After eighteen days of imprisonment, on the intervention of the Foreign Minister himself, he was suddenly released from prison.

As rumors of war between Japan and America became more and more pronounced, Kagawa redoubled his efforts to head off the conflict. In April, 1941, at the invitation of Christians in the United States, a group of eight Japanese Christians, headed by Dr. Kagawa, went to America. At Riverside, California, they spent a fortnight in discussion and prayer with seventeen representatives of the American churches. The members of both delegations were chosen by their respective National Christian Councils. During his visit, Kagawa himself addressed over three hundred meetings in the cause of peace. On his return home he appeared before the Japanese House of Peers to plead for a policy of mediation.

Suddenly on December 8, news came over the radio of a surprise attack by Japanese forces on the United States Fleet at Pearl Harbor. Kagawa listened in silence, tears streaming down his face. Fifty-three years old, half-blind and stricken by illness, he was to begin a period of anguish such as he had never experienced before.

Throughout the war years Kagawa took his stand against his nation's policy. For this he paid a heavy price. He was constantly under police surveillance and was arrested for short periods on two or three occasions. The one hundred and fifty books he had written by this time were all withdrawn from sale. Many were publicly burned. No publisher would accept a new manuscript. His schools were shut; his orphanages turned into military depots; his rural and town settlements closed down.

On the other hand, there was little restriction placed on his evangelistic work, at least during the early years of the war. Once he was permitted to spend a month of evangelism in Manchuria. On two occasions he was allowed to go to China for a preaching tour. However, toward the latter part of the war, he was forbidden to engage in any activity except preaching in his own church in Tokyo.

Kagawa's pacifism left him as distressed with American militarism as with that of his own country, and as the war increased in intensity, American bombing drew from him uncompromising condemnation. He thus came under attack from both East and West.

Toward the end of the war, when Japanese casualties were coming back in large numbers, the Government once more turned to Kagawa, as it had done in the days of the Tokyo earthquake. He was appointed chairman of the Government's war-time Relief Committeee, and later advisor to the Welfare Ministry, whose main concern was for the war sufferers and in particular those whose homes had been destroyed by bombing. This was work close to the heart of Kagawa, and once again he found an outlet for his compassion.

With the surrender of Japan, the nation entered a new era in its history. Militarism and dictatorship had been discredited. Peace and democracy were now to be the new pattern for the nation. But these were principles for which Toyohiko Kagawa had always stood. Thus, all of a sudden, Japanese leaders saw him as the most typical and indeed the most distinguished example of the way they must now pursue. Now from every side came appeals for his help.

The first appeal was from the Prime Minister himself. "Dr. Kagawa," he said,

Japan has been destroyed, not because we had not a sufficient army, but because we had suffered the loss of a good standard of morality and engaged in war. We need a new standard of ethics, like that of Jesus Christ. Buddhism can never teach us to forgive our enemies, nor can Shintoism. Only Jesus Christ was able to love his enemies. Therefore, Dr. Kagawa, if Japan is to be revived we need Jesus Christ as the basis of our national life. I want you to help me to put the love of Jesus Christ into the heart of the people.[1]

The Christian leader was deeply moved. He promised to serve in any way possible, except by actually taking office in the Government.

Within a month after the American occupation, Kagawa was already beginning again to be a public figure. He became advisor to the Department of Public Welfare, besides Welfare Advisor to Kobe City, managing director of the National Nutrition Society, and a member of the Committee set up by the Government to discuss the inauguration of a new parliamentary system and the holding of general elections.

[1] Cyril J. Davey, *Kagawa of Japan,* pp. 125-26.

He found himself involved at every level of the nation's reconstruction.

In September, 1945, Kagawa wrote an "Open Letter to General MacArthur" which was published in the daily newspaper, urging the American people to treat their enemy in Christian love. As a result he was called for an interview with the General and questioned as to how this might be put into practice. In reply he requested the General to extend his assistance to the homeless and hungry refugees, and to take steps to prevent a black market from developing.

One of the most significant events at this time was the arrival of a group of American church leaders in Japan. They were the very same men who had met at Riverside the year the war began. For two months they remained in Japan, meeting Christian and national leaders, and spreading goodwill among the populace.

When elections were held in the early part of 1946, Kagawa was urged by his friends to stand as a candidate for Parliament. He could have won the election with ease, but he refused saying, "I cannot do this. I must give my time to preaching." Accordingly, he gave himself to evangelistic campaigns across the nation, at a time when the people were receptive to the gospel as never before.

Often these tours were undertaken alone, but at times he teamed up with one or another of his American friends. Among these was his intimate friend, Dr. E. Stanley Jones, with whom he had shared a week's vigil of prayer in the days before the attack on Pearl Harbor. Five times they toured the country together. Halls and churches were packed to capacity; inquirers came by the hundreds.

It was in 1946, shortly after Emperor Hirohito had denounced his claim to divinity, that Kagawa received the greatest honor of his entire life. An official appeared at the

Kagawa household one day with a letter bearing the imperial seal. The Emperor wished to see Dr. Kagawa, that he might learn something of the Christian way. Kagawa was only supposed to take a half-hour for the interview, but the Emperor kept him for an hour and three-quarters as he listened intently and asked many questions. When the time came for Kagawa to leave, he drew from his robe a tattered copy of the Bible, the very book that had sustained him through the bitter years of the war. He opened it and began to read, "Whosoever would be great among you must be the servant of all." He went on to say that only through service can a man or nation be great.

On his seventieth birthday, three hundred leaders from all walks of life gathered in Tokyo to celebrate the occasion and do him honor. Speeches were made with all the ceremony and courtesy typical of the Japanese people. The old man's voice was choked with tears as he sought to reply.

It was the veteran's last public appearance. Worn down at last by chronic illness and unremitting service, he could resist no longer. He took to his bed and seldom left it thereafter. Finally, on April 23, 1960, he received his final summons from the King of kings and went to be with the Master whom he had served so faithfully and so diligently for over fifty-six years.

Toyohiko Kagawa was an individualist. He fitted into no pattern. He was a minister without a church, a doctor in philosophy who chose common laborers for his students, a Christian who was openly critical of the church, a pacifist who was prepared to stir up trouble.

Cyril J. Davey, in his biography of Kagawa, says,

His true significance lies in the fact that he would not allow any divorce between worship and service, and used every means at his disposal, including that of an untiring personal example, to show that evangelism must be matched by compassion, that the Church and its members must work out their faith in their daily life, and that devotion to Christ must drive men and women, at whatever personal cost, to serve those in need.[2]

[2] *Ibid.*, p. 147.

VI

Missionaries

*"And he said unto them, Go ye into all the world,
and preach the gospel to every creature."* MARK 16:15

THE GREAT COMMISSION given by our Lord is binding upon the
whole Christian Church. The Younger Churches, themselves the
products of missions, are called to be participants in the worldwide mission of the Church. They must unite their resources and
efforts with those of the Older Churches in a *partnership of
obedience* to meet the demands of a needy world.

Like their parent churches, the Younger Churches have been
somewhat slow in accepting the call to mission. With the exception of the churches of the Pacific Islands, only in recent years
have they begun to send forth missionaries to other lands in any
appreciable degree. Prophet Harris and Sadhu Sundar Singh
were pioneers ahead of their day to prick the conscience of the
growing Younger Churches. They had the courage to cross the
borders of their own native lands and take the gospel to neighboring peoples who lived in ignorance of the Savior's love.

11

William Wade Harris
of the Ivory Coast

In 1923, THE London office of the Wesleyan Missionary
Society was informed that the enacting of new language laws
by French Authorities had closed the small Methodist Church
at Grand Bassam in the Ivory Coast, West Africa. This was
a congregation consisting largely of Fanti-speaking clerks
who had migrated for trade purposes to the Ivory Coast.
Being familiar with French colonial law, the Reverend
J. W. Platt, superintendent of the Wesleyan Mission in
Dahomey, on request by the home office went to the Ivory
Coast to interview the government officials.

Little did Mr. Platt realize at the time how significant this
visit was destined to be. He had been ashore only a few hours
when a French lawyer, editor of a local newspaper, told him
of thousands of people in the Ivory Coast who had left their
pagan way of life and become disciples of Christ at the bidding of a mysterious African preacher whose name was
Harris. They had built scores of "meetinghouses" and met

regularly on Sundays to worship God. The lawyer said that though he had no particular interest in religion, in the course of his legal affairs he had come in contact with these people. They had actually offered him large sums of money to try to persuade him to go to France and bring out missionaries at their expense to instruct them in the Christian faith.

A high government official corroborated the lawyer's story. Being somewhat interested in religious matters, he had even appealed to one or two of his acquaintances in France to try to send out Christian workers but had failed in the attempt. He said to the Reverend Platt, "Where have you missionaries been for the past ten years? Away yonder are thousands of village people waiting for your help."

His official business completed, Mr. Platt went out to see the situation for himself. Sure enough, he found large groups of people, even whole clans, who had abandoned their former life at the bidding of a complete stranger. Some spoke of him as the "Big Man"; others called him "the Prophet." Fables of all kinds had grown up around his wondrous name. His acts of faith healing had grown in bulk enough to cover anything miraculous. He had foretold the European war—it was a punishment from God upon sinful Europe! He had set fire to a steamer anchored off Bassam because its crew was unloading cargo on Sunday. He had walked upon the water, saying he was going to England; but finding the white man's land a long way off, he had decided to return. He had proclaimed that fetishes were an abomination to the Lord of Heaven, and that his God was more powerful than these symbols and more to be feared. He had commanded men to destroy their secret charms, their animal skulls and bones that contained their hope for peace and protection. Ancestral shrines had been demolished also; ribald song-and-fetish dances, country folklore and agelong fairy tale, all went down under the sledge hammer of this irresistible traveling preacher. The powerful fetish priests, whose word was law among the tribes, had trembled before the fiery eye and confident assurance of this man. Men who tried to deceive him had been stricken with sickness or death. Had not a government official, having told the prophet to "move on," died shortly afterward? Had not a Roman Catholic priest who persecuted him suffered the crumbling of his church tower? . . . Such were the stories told.

The people had been won over by this man's confidence. Had Africa seen anything like it before? There were no doubts about him. He was a messenger from God Himself— he said so. He *knew* the will of God. Unlike the distant, unknowable god of their conception, this man's God lived, saw, acted, punished, protected, and could be talked to. The man talked to him, and he answered. Many knew it to their credit; others to their cost.

The Reverend J. W. Platt heard these things from a hundred eager Africans who claimed they had been eyewitnesses. They never tired of talking about their prophet. Whoever the man was, from wherever he came, and whatever he preached, he had certainly made an indelible impression on these humble people. The change in their faces was evidence of this fact. The strained, troubled look of the fear-ridden animist, known to Mr. Platt for many years in Dahomey, was not like the relaxed, peaceful countenances of the tellers of these strange stories. The new spirit of vigor and hope that they displayed was a part of the story. Some force which had not stopped at mere externals had contributed to the inner life of these people.

Who was this "prophet" who came and left so suddenly but had made such an impact upon the life and thought of the animist tribespeople of the French Ivory Coast? He was a man named William Wade Harris, a native of the neighboring land of Liberia. The exact date and place of his birth are not recorded, but he was probably born in a village near Cape Palmas somewhere between 1853 and 1855. We do know that he belonged to the Kru clan of the Grebo tribe, whose members had been evangelized under the remarkable ministry of Bishop J. C. Auer of the American Protestant Episcopal Mission. Making his headquarters in a central village named Cavalli, Bishop Auer mastered the Grebo language, reduced it to writing, translated several portions of the Bible, and produced a grammar and dictionary. He translated the Prayer Book and four hundred hymns into Grebo. In addition to his evangelistic work, he started a number of schools and taught many of the people to read and write. Cavalli furnished the greatest number of non-American Negroes to gain recognition by the American Negro governors of Liberia. A vice-president came from Cavalli.

William Harris grew up in the literate atmosphere created by Bishop Auer and his Bible. He learned to read both Grebo and English and avidly read everything that the bishop produced. He later attended the American Methodist Mission school at Cape Palmas, where he came in contact with the Reverend Jesse Lawry, African minister of the local Methodist Church. With Auer's books and Lawry's teaching, Harris grew up in an atmosphere saturated with the fear of the Lord. He nourished his spiritual life on portions of the Scriptures translated into Grebo and on the English Bible itself, until at the age of twenty-one he experienced a profound spiritual change.

Harris himself described this experience, saying, "I felt the Holy Spirit come upon me and change me at the moment of my conversion in the church." He ascribed this experience to the preaching of the Reverend Jesse Lawry, based on the words of the text of Revelation 2:4, 5, "That which I have against you is that you have abandoned your first love;

turn then from whence you have fallen; repent and do your former works, or else I will come to you and take away your candlestick from its place."

After several voyages up and down the west coast of Africa, William Harris, in keeping with tribal tradition, worked for some time as a bricklayer and then served for almost ten years in the mission school of his village, teaching elementary reading and writing.

During this period relations between the Grebo people and the Liberian government at Monrovia took a turn for the worse. The rulers were descendants of freed slaves who had been established in Liberia by conscience-smitten white folk in the United States. As such they were not regarded native to the country as were the Grebos; they were looked upon as foreigners who had taken over the administrative control of the land. At times the attitude of the ruling class in Monrovia—their air of superiority in particular—irked the feelings of the tribal people. The Grebos were racially a sensitive group and found themselves in a state of constant friction with the government. They actually felt that they could enjoy a larger measure of liberty if they lived in a recognized colony under some European nation or other. There were three separate uprisings between the years 1893 and 1910, and William Harris was caught up in these feelings of tribal loyalty and in the political movement that ensued. On several occasions he was guilty of hoisting a British Union Jack on his housetop and consequently became known in Liberia as "Old Man Union Jack."

During the uprising in 1910, William Harris went too far and was thrown into prison for several months. It was there that his prophetic mission began. Despondent, alone with his Bible, having struggled for liberty for his own little group and been defeated—how like those Hebrew prophets of whom he was reading! The oppression which his people suffered called for one who would cry out for free speech and liberty. Is it any wonder that a prophet was born?

In a trance there came to Harris a call to preach; the angel Gabriel hailed him as a prophet of God; he was anointed with the Spirit; he was told to obey the Great Commission. Immediately upon his release from prison he put his commission into force. He began to deliver his message to the people but was again imprisoned as a disturber of the peace. For the next two years or more he met with continued opposition; his preaching seemed to have little effect on the Liberians. It became clear that he would not be accepted as a prophet in his own country and that his mission would have to be fulfilled outside the borders of Liberia. Eventually in 1913, when he was close to sixty years of age, he made his way across the frontier to the Gold Coast and later to the French Ivory Coast. In the providence of God he was destined to become a missionary from the tiny Grebo tribe to the more populated neighboring tribes who had never heard the story of Christ.

A photograph of Harris taken about this time shows a well-built, muscular man of tall stature, with strongly marked features, a grey beard and moustache, dressed in a long white gown and an ample white turban. Around his shoulders and hanging down in front is a broad black band, and upon his breast there hangs a small cross. He walked barefoot and in his right hand carried a long bamboo walking staff with a crosspiece tied to it by a wisp of native grass. This he held aloft as a crude visual aid while telling the people that Christ died on the cross for their sins. He also carried a small, well-worn Bible and a crude bowl, made from a gourd shell, in which he carried water to baptize his converts. On his belt he wore a calabash containing dried seeds which he shook to keep rhythm for his hymns.

The message Harris proclaimed was as simple as his dress: there is one God, therefore destroy the objects of your pagan worship; there is one Savior who died upon the cross for men, therefore turn to him and be baptized. He taught the people the Lord's Prayer and the Ten Commandments, and to sing and praise God. His preaching was in pidgin English, interpreted into the local dialects by his faithful companion, Victor Tano. In all his messages he quoted extensively from the Bible as his sole authority.

When baptizing a convert, Harris made the candidate kneel and grasp with both hands the staff of his own bamboo cross. He then laid his Bible on the convert's head and said, "This is God's book. You must obey it." Then, in the name of the Trinity, he sprinkled upon the head water from his gourd.

The evangelist encouraged the people to work diligently and to obey their authorities. He forbade thieving and the use of alcohol. He asked that Sunday be considered as a day of rest and meditation. He tolerated polygamy but denounced adultery. He ordered all fetishes to be burned. When there was danger of his own bamboo cross being mistaken for a fetish, he would break it up, throw it away, and make another. He promised to those who followed his preaching a marvelous Beyond and assured his converts that by baptism they were purified.

Unlike the doubting Liberians, the people of the Ivory Coast gave heed to William Harris. They looked upon him as a prophet sent from God. They were convinced by his undaunted assurance and at the same time touched by his sincere humility. He knew he was commissioned by God, yet attached no importance to himself; he confessed himself an instrument in the hand of God. To put it in his own words, he was the "carpet on which Christ wiped his feet." The people thronged to hear him speak. They destroyed their fetishes and by the hundreds took baptism in the name of the Savior. Captain Paul Marty, French Government official serving in the Ivory Coast at the time, describes Harris' methods in these words:

The procedure of conversion of the "prophet" is always the same; he goes into a village, the crowds surround him; men on the right, women on the left. He then cries with a thunderous voice concerning the evil that the fetishes do them, and he orders the sorcerers to come and place themselves before him. He shows them his cross. These people are then seized with convulsions; they try to flee, but cannot; they roll on the ground screaming. They appear at this moment in a hypnotic state. Harris calms them and traces on their foreheads the sign of the cross with water, making them hold his cross. The sorcerers go off of their own will to break their idols. The village is baptized. The rumor spreads little by little that those who do not obey his moral advice are immediately punished, not only by the death given by the fetishes, but by the impossibility of committing the evil action that they proposed to do.[1]

It appears that Harris believed in and practiced faith healing as a part of his ministry. On several occasions cures of the sick were performed by him. However, he did not stress healing or any aspect of the miraculous. The legends that sprang up later about his many miraculous powers found their origin in the fertile imaginations of an illiterate people who had been completely captured by the man's impressive personality.

Though limited in intellect and education, the evangelist from Liberia was endowed with good common sense. When, according to his command, the people in village after village had destroyed their fetishes and swept away many of the ancient customs, some of his followers came to him anxiously to inquire what they were to do in case of illness. It had

[1] J. W. Platt, *An African Prophet,* pp. 60-61. Quoted by permission of the Student Christian Movement Press, London, England.

been their custom to go to the medicine man and obtain various herbs and concoctions over which he had uttered his magical formula and performed his ritual. What were they to do now that magic and ritual in such matters were taboo? A thoughtless leader might have forbidden the people to approach the medicine man under the new conditions of life, even for his helpful herbs. Harris told the people they might go to the medicine man and accept his herbs, but that they must not permit him to perform his ritual or even say the name of God over them.

It is interesting to note that William Harris would accept nothing from the people in consideration for his services, except their hospitality. He gratefully accepted their food and their offer to wash his clothes. When gifts were pressed upon him by chiefs and people, he straightaway distributed them to the poor. French officials who suspected that he might be profiting personally from his propaganda, inquired into the matter and were amazed when they discovered that the evangelist refused any sort of remuneration.

About the middle of 1914, "the Black Prophet" crossed into the British Gold Coast Colony and preached among the forest tribes of Apollonia. There the scenes were repeated which accompanied his preaching in the Ivory Coast. Thousands destroyed their fetishes and turned to the Living God during the few months Harris remained among them.

When Harris returned from Apollonia, he found the French governor of the Ivory Coast decidedly anxious about the mass movement which was taking place in the villages. War had broken out with Germany, and a good share of the colonial military forces had been shifted to the front in Europe. Native excitement or unrest was the one thing the governor feared. Thus in April, 1915, it was resolved, as a precautionary measure, to arrest the prophet and deport him. The story of this event, given in the words of the district officer commissioned to carry out the order, is touching indeed:

> I went to arrest the Old Man on the beach, where he was preaching and baptizing the crowds who listened to him.
>
> He was in the middle of his discourse when I arrived, followed by my men. My servant and cook followed from curiosity. I let him finish his sermon. . . . I waited until he had finished his baptizing. . . . Then I informed him that he must leave the Colony immediately. He did not struggle, nor scream out invective. He did not lose his dignity, nor did he give himself up to any grotesque demonstration. He came quietly. . . . But my servant and my cook wanted baptism by the man I was arresting, and they asked my permission. I had no objection, and they asked the Old Man. . . . Quietly, knowing he was being taken away by me, he baptized them.[2]

Partly on foot and partly by canoe, Harris was quietly escorted to the frontier of his native Liberia, nearly three hundred miles away, and forbidden to return. His missionary career ended as suddenly as it began.

The evangelist had been deported, but his baptized converts remained in village after village along the coast and in the interior. In less than two years, almost a hundred thousand people had been influenced by his preaching. Little bamboo and thatch churches had sprung up in scores of villages, and in each of these, in response to the advice of their prophet, the believers had appointed twelve apostles to manage the affairs of their church, and a preacher to lead the services. These men were almost wholly illiterate and repeated in their own way the message with which Harris had entrusted them. All remained in their occupations and gave voluntary service to their congregations.

All these churches were built by the "Harris Christians"

[2] *Ibid.*, p. 56.

with their own hands. Each church had its bell, hung in a small tower erected apart from the main building. Within, the church was furnished with rough benches made in the forest, with a little table at which the preacher stood, surrounded by the twelve apostles. The services were simple, rich in prayer, and interspersed with the singing, in pidgin English, of Christian hymns which they could not understand. Harris instructed his converts to hold daily morning prayers as well as evening hymn sings, a discipline which no doubt was mainly responsible for the nourishing of their spiritual lives.

Many eyewitnesses attested that the preaching of the Liberian missionary, in spite of all his limitations, had made a profound change in the lives of these people. One English trader, in describing the Harris movement to some friends, remarked in awe, "I was in Fresco when this prophet fellow arrived, and from a town of debased fetishism he changed it into one of nominal Christianity in three days." [3]

The Roman Catholic priests said of him, "This man Harris did more in three months in French West Africa than a host of missionaries could do in a hundred years." [4]

The movement inspired by William Harris was not without its trials and hardships. Having deported the evangelist, the French governor decided to crush the movement before it grew too strong. He ordered many of the churches to be destroyed by fire and issued a ban on all worship services. The reaction of these new converts to the trial of their faith was magnificent. They braved official wrath and openly held their services. In place of the bamboo and wattle meeting-houses they erected more attractive buildings and in some places constructed costly structures in hewn stone. In each church they placed an English or French Bible, which they could not read, confident in the word of their prophet that

[3] *Ibid.,* p. 34.
[4] *Ibid.,* p. 60.

one day God would send white missionaries who would unlock the book.

For ten long years these Christians waited. The outside world had heard little or nothing of this tremendous spiritual movement until, in 1923, the Reverend J. W. Platt visited the Ivory Coast and began to hear reports of the "Harris Christians."

Returning in 1924 to survey the situation, Mr. Platt was amazed both at the range of the movement William Harris had initiated and at the extent of the transformation it had produced. He was received in village after village with overflowing joy. Everywhere there were flags, torchlight processions, crowded churches, and excited people who hailed the new messenger of the gospel, whose coming Harris had foretold. "We have waited ten years for you," they said. Roman Catholic offers of help had been refused because the priests had not taken a strong stand against fetishism and had not consented to teach the people from "the Book."

The Wesleyan Missionary Society, though facing a deficit and limited in its personnel, courageously accepted the call to minister to the "Harris Christians." Within a year the mission had four missionaries and eight African ministers in the new field. The latter group came from the churches in French Dahomey where the Reverend Platt had been serving for the past five years. These workers were for the most part lay preachers with a minimum of education and training, but they were sincere, devoted, hardworking men who quickly identified themselves with the Ivory Coast Christians, learned the various dialects involved, and rendered valuable service in conducting worship services and instructing the new converts in basic Christian beliefs. Though in the interim ten-year period a good number of the people whom Harris baptized had turned back to their pagan ways, within the space of two years the Wesleyan Mission had over

32,000 names on its church registers and was ministering to a Christian community of over 45,000 people.

The task of organizing, instructing, and nurturing so many new "babes in Christ" was indeed one of gigantic proportions. William Harris had achieved a great deal during his brief ministry, but there were serious limitations in the whole movement. The Reverend Platt and his small band of workers very judiciously sought to build upon the good foundation that had been laid, but at the same time sought to correct the mistakes and supply the deficiencies.

In the first place, the message of "the Prophet" had its limitations. Though it was strong enough to deliver the people from the bonds of fetishism and all its accompanying fears, it was quite evident that it had in many cases merely substituted another fear of a higher level—the fear of a God of wrath. In his preaching Harris had stressed the judgments of God. There was little emphasis on the filial relationship to God the Father, that tenderness and love, that sharing of our life by God which is the basis of the Christian message and the only hope of its real attainment. A new message was necessary, new truth whose qualities were more personal, more transforming, and more energizing than the word Harris gave and, perhaps, than he himself knew. The magnificent message of Harris to the Ivory Coast people lifted them to a higher plane, a plane where one God lived; but their conception of that God, his character and his ways, and their relationship to him needed to be intensified and extended before it could redeem all areas of their living.

Then there was the problem of illiteracy. New Christians cannot grow in an intellectual vacuum. The people had the Bible, but it was in a foreign language, and the people could not even read their own. In a meeting with fifty-two of the Harris "preachers," the Reverend Platt asked those who could read to raise their hands. There were only two! In one church he found "the Book" carefully placed on the table as usual, but when he opened it he discovered it contained advertising of patent medicines! Poor people, how were they to know? They had done their best; but ignorant and illiterate religion is always dangerous. Already the new movement was failing to hold the youth, a new generation which had not known "the Prophet." With the ultimate dying off of the generation contemporaneous with Harris, the movement would have undoubtedly died also.

The missionaries tackled the task of education with a most ambitious scheme. They started a good number of primary schools in the villages, in addition to four central schools and a Bible school. Children were given a basic training in the vernacular with a strong emphasis on religious education, using the Bible as a text book. A program of adult literacy was drawn up to enable older people to read the Bible. A manual for village catechists was produced to help train lay preachers for the regular Sunday services. A few major tribal dialects were reduced to writing, and with the assistance of the British and Foreign Bible Society, several portions of Scripture were translated and published. In the central Bible school at Dabou, the most promising young men were trained and sent out as pastors to various congregations. In all this program the people responded with a degree of zeal and ability that amazed the missionaries and teachers.

One of the major problems to be tackled was that of polygamy, which has been a constant challenge to the skill and patience of the African Church. As mentioned before, William Harris strongly condemned adultery, but he permitted the practice of polygamy among his followers. No doubt he was wise in this policy, for it was the only possible approach he could have taken at the time. With a mass movement upon his hands, and the custom of polygamy widely prevalent among the tribespeople, to have insisted upon monogamy at one swift stroke would have created havoc in many a home and in the whole social structure. It is quite possible that "the Prophet's" sway over the people would have been strong enough to command their implicit obedience and, had he ordered it, would have led to the sending away of thousands of unfortunate African women from their polygamous husbands. But many children would have suffered, and it would have wrecked all clan life and in turn might have utterly destroyed the cohesion of the movement itself.

The missionaries realized that polygamy could not be perpetuated as a regular practice in the Church, but at the same time they were wise enough to see that the solution to the problem would require tact and patience on their part and a gradual growth in grace and knowledge of the Lord Jesus Christ on the part of the new Christians. They instituted a system of training for the girls as well as the boys and placed great emphasis on the Christian ideals of marriage and the home. Their slogan was not so much "one man, one wife," which is the European expression of the marriage duty, but "all children must have one father and mother," which is the African way of saying the same thing. It is the complete blood-unity of the family group which polygamy does not attain.

There was the question of an adequate hymnology for the new churches. William Harris had laid great stress upon music in his preaching campaigns but had taught his converts only a few English hymns, which were unintelligible to them. They sang these Western hymns with a typical African beat, and so mutilated the words and tunes that they were often completely unrecognizable. The Reverend J. W. Platt and his colleagues inspired the people to express their new Christian experience in their own words and use their own native tunes. At first the villagers opposed the suggestion, for most of their music was connected with the old fetish dances. But when the missionaries showed them how an ancient paramount chief, David, had composed his own songs to praise the King of Heaven, the tribespeople soon responded and in the course of time developed an indigenous and meaningful hymnology for their worship services.

Last of all, the missionaries added to the Harris communities that high peak of worship and fellowship that the Liberian evangelist had completely neglected, the celebration of the Lord's Supper. In time this sacrament came to have great meaning to the new communities in the Ivory Coast, for it is at the Lord's Table where life and religion meet in one family. There the Harris clans merged into worldwide homage to Christ and became a part of that universal fellowship which constitutes the Christian Church.

In the fall of 1926, Mr. P. Benoit of the Wesleyan Mission in the Ivory Coast, accompanied by William Harris' Negro interpreter, Victor Tano, journeyed to Cape Palmas in Liberia to pay "the Prophet" a visit. It had been almost twelve years since Harris had been deported from his scene of missionary labor. They found the old preacher, now over seventy years of age and a widower, living in the modest home of his daughter and surrounded by his grandchildren who were all attending the Methodist Mission school. When he discovered who his visitors were, his eyes lit up with joy, and he began to question them about the welfare of his children in the Ivory Coast. Were they still worshiping the Living God? Had they gone back to their fetishes and old ways? Had missionaries come to instruct the converts?

Harris told Mr. Benoit that he had attempted on eight different occasions to reenter the Ivory Coast but each time had been turned back at the border by the French authorities. On one of the occasions he was imprisoned for a brief period. He still traveled hundreds of miles on foot, preaching and baptizing those who would receive him, but without any great success among his own people.

A few years later William Harris, missionary extraordinary, died at his home in Cape Palmas. His death attracted little attention among his fellow countrymen, but thousands of earnest Christians in the Ivory Coast remembered him as their spiritual father with deep gratitude and respect.

Harris brought into the field of Christian endeavor something different from the conventional work of Christian missions. He stood before his people, not as one by any Society or backed by European prestige, but as a "man sent from God" with a message for his people; and his people listened and obeyed. Though Harris was foreign to the Ivory Coast and had to speak in a foreign language through interpretation, still he was a Negro, born in West Africa, and Africa understands her own whatever the vocabulary. He had a racial heritage common to his hearers; he had an individual experience of the fear of the invisible, which they felt. He was, like his compatriots, deeply religious and needed a living God who spoke in terms of his life. But, unlike the people to whom he came, he was free, hopeful, enthusiastic, dogmatic in his definite ideas of the Unseen. He claimed to know, to have had an experience of an active God.

Modern missions supply no case of such multitudes being brought to God in so short a time by the preaching of a single man. In the past God has often used strange messengers, but it is doubtful if a man of such severe limitations was ever the instrument of so widespread a movement.

12

Sadhu Sundar Singh
of India

WITHOUT DOUBT THE most famous and best loved servant
of the cross in India was Sadhu Sundar Singh, regarded by
many as the greatest Christian that India thus far has
produced. To this day he is considered the epitome of
Christian life and example.

Sundar Singh (meaning "the beautiful lion") was a Sikh
by birth. Sikhism is one of the world's youngest faiths,
originating in the Punjab section of India in the latter part
of the fifteenth century. It is an interesting example of
conscious syncretism, being originally a blend of the best in
Hinduism and Islam. It sought to worship the one God
without idolatry and caste. Its basic conviction, monotheism,
is drawn from Islamic sources, while its other major doctrines
are taken, with little if any change, directly from Hinduism.
Because of opposition and persecution from both Muslims
and Hindus, the Sikhs early in their history took up the
sword to defend their faith and soon developed into an

organized military power, determined to avenge the many wrongs inflicted upon them. Pride of race, love of arms, and a fanatical religious zeal are outstanding characteristics of these people.

Sundar Singh was born on September 3, 1889, in the village of Rampur in Northern India. His father was a wealthy landowner who brought him up in the lap of luxury. His mother was a deeply religious person, who often said to him, "Son, you must not be careless and worldly like your brothers. You must seek peace of soul and love religion, and some day you must become a 'sadhu' " (religious ascetic).

So frequently did Sundar hear such words as these from his mother's lips that he never contemplated any other life than that of which she spoke. Her sudden death, when he was fourteen years of age, only served to heighten his religious ambition.

After his mother's death, Sundar Singh threw himself into his quest for peace of heart with great zeal. The sacred books of the Sikhs and Hindus and even the Koran of the Muslims were all ceaselessly read and searched. Often when his family lay asleep, Sundar sat poring over the pages of one of these books. Many verses and passages he learned by heart, and yet all his increasing knowledge only produced a deeper unrest of his soul.

At that time, Sundar Singh was enrolled in an American Presbyterian mission school and came into contact with the Christian faith for the first time in his life. But his deep inbred reverence for his own religion, almost amounting to fanaticism, turned him against this new and strange religion. Soon he became the ringleader of the boys who hated Christianity in the school. One day, in the presence of some of the students, he tore up the pages of a New Testament and threw them into a fire.

When his father heard of the incident, he chided Sundar

for his rashness and insisted that the Bible was a good book which he should have returned to the missionary rather than treat it with disrespect. But so strong were Sundar's feelings at that time that he could not listen to reason. On one occasion, when the shadow of a Christian missionary fell across his body, he spent a whole hour in washing away the pollution.

Sundar Singh later spoke of this period as one of the most trying of his life, for he had come to the end of his own religion without discovering the "shanti" (peace) he was in search of, and his deep-rooted hatred of Christianity prevented him from even looking into the Christian sacred book for the "pearl of great price."

Finally the thought entered his mind that there might be some ray of hope in the despised book he had so furiously destroyed; and so at last he took the New Testament and began to read. Soon he was reading such marvelous words as those in Matthew 11:28 and John 3:16. The words arrested him, and as he read the story of the Cross, his wonder grew. But still the anguish of his soul remained.

At last Sundar Singh felt he must put an end to the struggle. Resolved that he would seek peace before dawn—either in this world or the next—he arose at 3 A.M. one morning and, after taking a cold bath, began to pray. "If there be any God let him show me the way of salvation; if not, then I will commit suicide by placing myself on the railway track." (The express train passed right behind his home at five o'clock every morning.)

What happened can best be told in the words of Sundar Singh himself. In a printed testimony he writes:

Up to 4:30 no answer came. Presently there came a light in my room. In that light the beloved and glorious face of Christ appeared, and showing His wounded hands in which the nail-prints were clearly visible, He said: "Why do you persecute Me?

Behold, I gave my life upon the cross for you, and that the world might have salvation." Upon my hearing this His words sank like lightning into my heart. I immediately became filled with joy, and I was changed for all eternity. Although Christ disappeared after speaking thus to me, the peace He gave me will remain forever. This was not imagination. If Buddha or Krishna had shown himself, it would have been imagination, for I worshipped them; but for Christ to show Himself, Him whom I hated, is a miracle, and clear proof that He is a living Christ. Neither was it a dream, for no one can see a dream after taking a cold bath, and a dream cannot completely change a life. This was a great reality! [1]

At first Sundar Singh's father did not take seriously his account of the vision and his determination to follow Christ. But when Sundar cut off his long hair, which is a sign of the Sikh religion, he knew that his son was really in earnest. He attempted to dissuade him from becoming a Christian by using every means of pleading and reasoning. He appealed to Sundar's family pride; he appealed to his religious loyalty; he reminded him of his precious mother's dying wish; he reminded him of the high estate to which he had been born and the noble prospects that lay before him. But Sundar, though just a youth of fifteen, remained strong in his new faith.

Seeing that the father's attempts had failed, an honored uncle sought to make a fresh appeal to young Sundar. One day he took him to his large house and led him to a deep cellar below the main building. There he opened a large safe and revealed to the boy such wealth as he had never seen before. Rolls of bank notes and piles of precious jewels lay before his eyes. His uncle besought him not to disgrace the family name by becoming a Christian, and taking his turban

---

[1] Mrs. Arthur Parker, *Sadhu Sundar Singh—Called of God,* p. 112.

from his own head, he laid it on Sundar's feet, as the last and humblest supplication he could make, with the words, "All these shall be yours if you will remain with us."

Sundar felt this temptation keenly, for not only did the sight of such riches dazzle his eyes, but his heart was deeply moved by the humble condescension of his uncle. But the memory of the vision of the thorn-crowned Savior and of the tender voice of his Master kept him steadfast even in the face of this severe temptation.

From then on tender persuasion turned to open hostility. Sundar's father made it plain to him that he was no longer a son but an outcast. His food was served to him outside the house just as if he belonged to the "untouchables," and he was made to sleep on the verandah. Finally, all the pent-up anger of his father was let loose upon him, and he was told that he must leave the home for good. Before sunrise the following day, he was cast out with nothing but the thin clothes he wore and enough money to take him a short journey by train. Homeless, friendless, and utterly destitute, Sundar turned his back on the home of his childhood.

He took the train to the small town of Ropur, where there was a little colony of Christians, and made his way to the house of the kind Indian pastor and his wife. This was in the providence of God, for very soon after his arrival he fell violently ill, and a doctor had to be called in. Then it became known that a deadly poison had been mixed in the food given him before leaving home. The physician pronounced the case as hopeless and departed with the expectation to come in the morning for the funeral.

Sundar lay in mortal pain with blood flowing from his mouth, but somehow he just could not believe that death at that time was according to the purpose of God. So he began to pray with all his remaining strength. When morning came he was still alive, though exceedingly weak.

When the doctor came, he was amazed to find the boy alive. So deeply impressed was he that he took a copy of the New Testament and began to study it. As a result the physician himself became a believer in Christ and later became a missionary to Burma.

This doctor was Sundar Singh's first convert, who set the pattern of his whole life—that of a soul winner for Christ.

When Sundar was strong enough to travel, he made the short journey to Ludhiana to the home of some American missionaries. While there, several attempts were made by his relatives to get him away, and violence was used on one of these occasions, so that the police had to be called in to quell the disturbance.

But the most trying experience came to Sundar when his aged father appeared to make one last attempt to draw his son back into his native faith. The old man spoke of the great love of his mother, the happy days of his childhood, and the loneliness of the home without him. Sundar's tears flowed down his cheeks while a mighty struggle went on in his heart. But when he remembered the sacrifice his Savior had made for him, it gave him strength to make the last great sacrifice for his Lord.

After these events it became necessary for Sundar to seek refuge from his enemies, so he went on to Simla where other missionaries gave him shelter. Finally on September 8, 1905, on his sixteenth birthday, he took the final step of Christian baptism and publicly declared his faith in Jesus Christ.

Sundar's heart now became filled with a burning desire to make known to others the Savior for whom he had forsaken all. He had long felt drawn to the life of a sadhu; in fact, this is what his mother had always wanted him to be. Now he decided that he would be a sadhu for Christ.

"Sadhu" is a Sanskrit word and literally means "straight" and hence "pure" or "holy." In religious parlance it denotes a Hindu ascetic, who renounces the world with all its pleasures and devotes himself completely to matters of the spirit. The life of the sadhu is characterized by rigorous discipline including celibacy, poverty, fasting, and self-mortification. The devotee adopts the saffron robe and wanders homeless from place to place, depending entirely upon hospitality of the people for his food and shelter. To a Hindu the sadhu is the ideal of self-renunciation and saintliness and therefore one to whom he must always bow in reverence and humility.

Sundar Singh decided that he would christianize the concept of the sadhu by renouncing himself and the world for the sake of others in an untiring search for lost men. He would remain "in the world but not of it." He would "endure all things" and be "all things to all men" for the glory of Christ. He would travel from place to place preaching Christ, without any expectation of financial remuneration. If food were offered to him he would partake of it; otherwise he would go hungry. He would sleep in a house if he were invited to do so; otherwise he would sleep under a tree or in a cave. He would depend not so much on the generosity of men, but on the faithfulness of the Heavenly Father.

His mind fully made up, Sundar Singh took steps to fulfill his vow. He quickly disposed of all his personal belongings, and on October 6, 1905, about a month after his baptism, he adopted the simple saffron robe that was to mark him for the rest of his days as one committed to a religious life. Without purse or any visible means of support, but with faith in his heart and his New Testament in his hand, Sadhu Sundar Singh set out in his ministry of serving and suffering that was to leave an indelible imprint on the church and people of his beloved India.

The young sadhu decided he would make Acts 1:8 the pattern of his ministry. He would be a witness for Christ, beginning in Jerusalem and going on to the ends of the earth. Though but a boy of sixteen, his intense love for his Lord caused him to choose as his first field of service his own village, from which he had been driven only a few months previously. He returned to Rampur, and there in every street and from house to house he bore witness to the power of the Living Savior and his new-found peace.

From there he walked to surrounding villages, fearlessly testifying to the people everywhere of salvation in Christ, then continued his way through many other towns of the Punjab, and worked his way up toward Kashmir and Afghanistan. This was a long and extremely arduous journey, and, unaccustomed to the hardships of a sadhu life, Sundar suffered severely from the cold and privations of the way. Moreover, his work was difficult for the response was poor, and he was often driven hungry and helpless from villages where he sought to preach.

One particularly dark night, after a very discouraging day, the sadhu found a cave where he spread his blanket and lay down to sleep. When daylight came and he opened his eyes, there was a leopard, curled up and asleep, on part of his blanket. The sight almost paralyzed him with fear. Once outside the cave, he could only thank God for sparing his life.

On another occasion, he awakened from sleep to find a large cobra sharing the warmth of his blanket. His first impulse was to jump up and run, but then he inwardly calmed himself, quietly arose, shook the cobra off the blanket, and softly walked away. He couldn't afford to lose a second blanket!

Sundar Singh's labors were not without fruit. Everywhere he found those who would give attention to his message, and several who listened were led to faith in Christ as their personal Savior.

Once, while traveling through a jungle area, he suddenly

became ill with a high fever and severe internal pains. He sank helpless in the path. With great difficulty a fellow traveler succeeded in getting him to the house of a European forest officer some miles away, and there he was finally nursed back to health. The host was a man who cared nothing for religion, but day by day he saw the Christ-like life of the sadhu and listened to his testimony. As a result he surrendered himself to Christ and became a truly converted man. Thus was Sundar Singh's illness used for the salvation of his European host.

One day when the young sadhu arrived at a village, he sat down upon a log and, wiping the perspiration from his face, started singing a Christian hymn. Soon a crowd gathered, but when they discovered that the stranger was a Christian, many of the people became angry. One man jumped up and dealt him such a severe blow that he fell to the ground, badly cutting his cheek and hand. Without a word Sundar rose and bound up his bleeding hand and, with blood running down his face, prayed for his enemies and spoke to them of the love of Christ. As a result, one of the bystanders was converted, and the very man who had struck Sundar Singh to the ground sought the forgiveness of the Savior and openly confessed Christ by baptism.

On another occasion, when the sadhu was passing through a dense forest, four robbers suddenly rushed on him with their knives. Unable to protect himself and believing the end had come, he bowed his head to receive the blow. This unexpected conduct caused the men to hesitate and to inquire instead who he was. Sundar told them he was a Christian sadhu, opened his New Testament, and began to introduce Christ to them. The leader of the gang then took Sundar to his cave, prepared food for him, and begged him to tell him more of this man Jesus Christ. Tears of penitence streamed down the face of the robber as he heard the wonderful story of Christ and the thief on the cross. Then he said to the sadhu, "Come with me; I have something to show you."

He led Sundar to a nearby cave where he pointed to a heap of human bones. "These are my sins," he cried. "Tell me, is there any hope for a sinner like me?"

The sadhu assured him of the forgiveness and mercy of the Savior, and as the two knelt together in the cave, the penitent thief sobbed out a prayer to God. The man was gloriously converted and accompanied Sundar to the nearest mission station, where he openly confessed his new faith by accepting Christian baptism. Moreover, through the witness of their leader the other three robbers were also won to Christ, gave up their old life, and took to honest occupations. Thus did the sadhu turn personal danger into an opportunity to lead four sinners to the Savior.

Sundar Singh's intense devotion and love for Christ caused him to turn his face toward the vast mountainous regions of the Himalayas where Christ had never, or rarely, been preached. And so in 1908, at the youthful age of nineteen, he crossed over into the closed land of Tibet. On foot he trekked from village to village, incessantly preaching the good news of Jesus Christ.

This proved to be a major decision in his ministry, for from then on Sundar Singh considered himself God's messenger to Tibet. Beginning in the year 1911, each year during the hot summer months in India he returned to Tibet to continue his ministry among that most needy people. He also made treks into Nepal, Bhutan, and Sikkim.

It was in these unfriendly countries that Sundar Singh suffered most for his Lord. Once in the town of Ilom, Nepal, he was arrested for preaching in the public square and was thrown into the common prison, to spend his days and nights with murderers and thieves. When news came to the officials that the Christian sadhu was preaching to the inmates, they were infuriated and dragged him to the public market for punishment. Here he was stripped of his clothing and made to sit on the earth. His feet and hands were fastened in stocks, and a number of leeches were thrown over his naked body. These immediately fastened upon him and began to suck his lifeblood.

Through the long night he agonized, growing hourly weaker with loss of blood. But when morning came he was still alive. Suddenly the joy of the Lord filled his heart and he began to sing and praise God. When his persecutors saw the sadhu's tranquil face, they were filled with superstitious dread and hurriedly set him free.

This experience had made him so weak that he fell unconscious, but some secret believers carried him to their home and nursed him back to health. To his death the sadhu carried the scars of this punishment.

On another occasion, at a town called Rasar in Tibet, he was arraigned before the head lama and condemned to death. He was stripped of his clothes and thrown into a dry well, the top being firmly fastened over his head. He fell on a mass of human bones and rotting flesh. Wherever he laid his hands they met putrid flesh, while the odor almost poisoned him. In the dark, without food and water, Sundar felt he could not last very long.

On the third night he suddenly heard a grating sound overhead. Someone was opening the locked lid of his dismal prison. Then a voice called out telling him to take hold of the rope being lowered. With all his remaining strength he grasped the rope and was strongly but gently pulled up from the vile place into the fresh air above.

When news came to the lama the next day that the Christian sadhu was well and preaching again, Sundar was again arrested and brought to the judgment seat. Questioned as to what had happened, he told the story of his marvelous

escape. The lama flew into a fit of rage and declared that
someone must have stolen the key and gone to his rescue;
but when a search was made for the key, it was found on his
own belt. In amazement and fear he pleaded with the sadhu
to leave the city and never come back, lest some great dis-
aster should come upon himself and his people.

From the year 1917, Sundar Singh's fame began to spread
widely. Every day fresh invitations reached him from all
directions, and out of them grew a great evangelistic tour
which took him not only all across India, but also to Ceylon,
Burma, the Federated Malay States, China, and Japan.
Thousands flocked to his meetings everywhere. Often the
day's work began so early and continued so late that he
had scarcely time to eat.

October 1919 was one of the greatest months in Sundar
Singh's life. Upon return from his annual trip to Tibet he
visited his own village of Rampur and spent a few days with
his aged father. There he was received with honor and much
affection, and after fourteen years of being an outcast from
his own home, he had the inexpressible joy of leading his dear
father to faith in Jesus Christ. Sundar left his father's house
radiant with joy to pursue his journey south and west.

Not long after this, Sundar Singh's father sealed his reunion with his son by sending him passage money to Europe,
in order that he might have the desire of his heart and carry
the gospel to the nations of the West.

Almost the entire year of 1920 was spent in an extensive
evangelistic campaign that took him through England, the
United States, and Australia. Here again thousands flocked
to hear his message and many turned to Christ. At a meeting
of the Church Missionary Society in Albert Hall in London,
ten thousand people were present and many listened from
outside, while at the meeting of the London Missionary
Society at Queen's Hall, hundreds could not obtain admis-

sion. On one occasion the sadhu occupied the pulpit of Dr. Jowett at Westminster. In the United States, leading pastors welcomed him to their pulpits; university and seminary presidents invited him to address their student bodies. Among the places where Sundar Singh spoke were the Marble Collegiate Church in Manhattan, Hartford Theological Seminary in Hartford, and Union Theological Seminary in New York. Everywhere the newspapers published résumés of his career, reports of his work, and discussions of his views on Western luxury and materialism.

The sadhu's Christ-like demeanor, his winsome personality, and his sincere messages made a lasting impression upon young and old alike. At one meeting in the United States, a small child of three sat in the front row. All through his address this little girl scarcely took her eyes from the sadhu's face. As he sat down, the audience was deeply moved when a clear childish treble voice was heard to ask, "Is he Jesus?"

In 1922, the sadhu made a second tour to the West, preaching extensively in England, Switzerland, Germany, Sweden, Norway, Denmark, and Holland.

The spiritual results of Sundar Singh's evangelistic tours were manifold. Many who were nominal in the Christian faith became genuine disciples of the Master. Earnest Christians were challenged to a life of greater simplicity and devotion. Those who were lukewarm about foreign missions became enthusiastic supporters of the mission of the Church.

When Sundar Singh returned to India after his visit to the West, his health began steadily to decline. For seventeen years he had given himself without stint to the work of preaching the gospel. In the earlier years of his ministry he often went without food; many nights he slept under a tree or in a cave. On several occasions he was beaten and imprisoned. As his fame began to spread, he was welcomed wherever he went, and there was no longer any difficulty about food and shelter. But the pressure of publicity and the strain of a crowded schedule began to take their toll. Even his robust constitution began to give way under the exacting demands made upon it. After the year 1922, he was often ill. Once he had to cancel a tour because of a hemorrhage. Twice he suffered a slight heart attack. He had trouble with one of his eyes and had to undergo an operation. As a result he was forced to cut his speaking schedule and accept invitations only as his health permitted.

By the grace of God however, Sundar Singh turned his burden into a blessing. Realizing that he could no longer travel extensively to proclaim the name of the Savior, he devoted himself to the ministry of writing. He produced several books which were translated into forty languages and had a wide circulation. Over 162,000 copies of his books were sold in the Danish language alone. From the royalties on those publications he was able to buy an old mission bungalow and live in relative comfort.

But soon the desire to preach took hold of the sadhu once again. The call of Tibet kept coming back to him. In April 1929, in spite of poor health and against the advice of his friends, he started out again for the land that had captured his heart. It proved to be the last earthly journey of this great man of God. He was never seen again. To this day not a trace of him has been found.

What happened to the Christian sadhu? Perhaps he became ill and crawled off into some cave to die. Perhaps an avalanche on some high Himalayan pass swept him away and buried him in an ocean of snow. Perhaps he was martyred for preaching the gospel.

What was the secret of Sadhu Sundar Singh's unique and effective ministry? Without doubt it was the fact that he allowed the gospel to be reflected in all its pristine simplicity and purity without taint by historical accretions and cultural impositions from abroad. He was thoroughly Christian and at the same time thoroughly Indian. He took the best in Indian culture and baptized it into the Christian life. He took the old ideal of renunciation and spiritualized it, so that men saw in him a reflection of the great renunciation of Christ himself—not seeking suffering for suffering's own sake, as is the case with Hindu asceticism, but enduring it with cheerful acceptance as being the will of God for him. He brought with him into his Christian life the Indian concepts of mysticism, meditation, and devotion, and consecrated them all to the service of his Master. The result was not merely a fusion of Christianity and Sikhism but a fresh and powerful presentation of genuine biblical Christianity.

Sundar Singh became a sadhu because he believed that God had called him to this method of service for him, and because he believed that this was a pattern of life that would be meaningful to the people of India. He utterly rejected the idea that there was any intrinsic and special holiness in the life of the sadhu. He was convinced that his people must see the Christian life in an Indian setting; that they must hear the Christian message through an Indian medium. He often told this story to illustrate:

A Brahman priest was carried to a railway platform after he had fainted in an overcrowded, overheated train. When someone brought a cup of water from the refreshment room in the container that was provided there, the priest waved it away in horror. But when a companion appeared with the Brahman's own brass bowl filled with water he drank it greedily.

Sundar Singh argued: "That is what I am always telling my Christian friends. We are offering Christianity in a Western cup and India rejects it. But when we offer the

Water of Life in an Eastern bowl, then our people will recognize it and take it gladly."

His preaching was characterized by simplicity coupled with sincerity. He lost no time in flowery speech and wasted no words on fine phrases. He was direct, clear, concise, and always spoke in great earnestness. His addresses portrayed a calm and glowing faith in God, so that it was impossible to hear him without realizing that here was one to whom God was real and intimate. He made his messages come alive by the use of vivid and often piquant illustrations drawn from his own experiences, while he invariably pressed home his points with unforgettable similes and parables. The great theme of all his preaching was Christ. He took great delight in pointing people to the Cross, for there he himself found peace and forgiveness and could speak with authority of the power of that Cross to save others.

In preaching to non-Christians, the sadhu never attacked their religion or used unbrotherly terms of reproach. He was convinced that religion is not a matter of argument but of experience. He fearlessly testified to his own failure, after long and painful search, to find peace and joy apart from God's great offer of redemption in Jesus Christ. He sought to draw non-Christians to the feet of Christ, not by logic or philosophy, but by the inspiration which comes from the simple yet powerful witness to God, the redeemer from sin.

Sundar Singh's picturesque appearance added to the appeal of his message. He was tall and well built, with a neatly trimmed beard, clad in a flowing saffron robe with a scarf of the same color thrown across his shoulders. On his bare feet he wore simple sandals. His face, with its serenity and radiance, reminded his listeners of the traditional portrait of our Lord.

He was a true Christian mystic. Things of the spiritual life were more real to him than those of the temporal. He saw the hand of his heavenly Father in even the most simple details of life. Long hours of communion with his Lord alternated with long days of toil among his fellowmen. A consuming passion to seek people which gave him no respite from his labors was balanced by a deep devotion and love for his Savior that filled his heart with peace and even shone in his face.

As a Sikh boy in rural surroundings, Sundar Singh had come to believe implicitly in the supernatural. His own temperament, with the long periods of meditation and prayer in which he engaged, only served to confirm his early beliefs. It was easy for him to see the miraculous in all experiences of life. He lived constantly in a land of dreams, visions, and miracles, so that often he was unable to distinguish between the imaginations of his inner mind and the actual happenings in the external world. He was inclined to believe that his dreams and visions had actually occurred in life and not merely taken place in his own mind. Sometimes this tendency caused confusion among his hearers; some sincerely questioned the veracity of his stories. When Sundar Singh began to realize that the narration of such "miracles" in his sermons detracted from his gospel message instead of aiding it, he scrupulously avoided weaving them into his addresses.

He had one magnificent obsession: to be like the One whom he loved and served so intensely. Christ was his constant ideal and example. He even rejoiced in suffering and hardship, because he felt that all such experiences served to identify him with the One who had suffered so much for him. Only through suffering could he understand the meaning of the Cross and come into intimate communion with the Savior. As a result, he gained a greater degree of saintliness than most followers of Christ ever achieve. In simplicity of living, purity of conduct, and such Christian graces as humility, gentleness and patience, he left behind a magnificent example.

One time, at least, this obsession carried him to an extreme. When he was twenty-four years of age, he decided to under- take a fast of forty days as his Lord had done. In the seclusion of a dense forest infested with wild animals, he sought to carry out his vow. After many days of fasting he became so weak that he slumped to the ground, unable to move. Two bamboo cutters found him in that state and, making a simple stretcher with his blanket and two bamboo poles, carried him to a nearby village where some Christians nursed him back to health. He was so weak that he could not even speak for a day or two; only after a week or so could he eat any solid food. How long he actually carried on the fast no one knows for certain. One reliable source estimates that the fast probably lasted for twenty-three days.

Another of Sundar Singh's characteristics was his ecumeni- cal spirit. Just a few years after his conversion, Bishop Lefroy of the Anglican Church sent Sundar to study theology in St. John's Divinity School in Lahore with a view to ordination. When the question arose as to whether Sundar would be free to preach in any Christian Church and to receive Communion there, the bishop told him frankly that this would not be permitted. He could only minister in the churches of the Anglican communion. The young student felt that this was not in accordance with the universal charac- ter of Christ's Church. So after much thought and prayer, he left the Divinity School, having been there less than eight months.

Like John Wesley, Sundar Singh looked upon the world as his parish, and he preached everywhere and to all who would give heed to his message. He felt at home in any denomination, in any church. During his trip to Europe and the United States he ministered with equal freedom to Quakers, Baptists, and Anglicans. "Sects are strange, un- necessary things," he commented. "There is one God; why have so many creeds? Peace and quiet come from knowing Christ. Why cause dissension?"

The name of Sadhu Sundar Singh is still a household word in thousands of homes in India. And to this day, when an evangelist wants to describe a real Christian, he points to this disciple of the Master as the most perfect example India has yet produced.

VII
Martyrs

*"Be thou faithful unto death, and I will
give thee a crown of life."* REVELATION 2:10

THE YOUNGER CHURCHES have been established at great cost.
Their members have not only had to face prejudice and persecution; some have had to face death.

Kartar Singh and the Sohn family are just a few among the
thousands of Christians in many lands who laid down their lives
for the cause of Christ. Even before the first missionaries arrived
in Korea, over ten thousand Catholic Christians had been martyred at the command of a tyrant. During the early days of
persecution in Japan, thousands of Christians were burned,
crucified, buried alive, subjected to every form of torture that
barbaric cruelty could devise. During the Boxer Rebellion in
China at the turn of this century, approximately sixteen thousand Chinese Christians suffered martyrdom because of their
faith. Even in recent years hundreds of African Christians have
suffered violent deaths at the hands of Mau Mau warriors and
Congolese rebels.

But let us remember, "The blood of martyrs is the seed of the
Church."

13
Kartar Singh
of India

SOME SERVANTS OF the Cross lived to a ripe old age and served their Master faithfully and effectively for many years. They were great in the message they preached and in the mission they performed. Others were martyred in the prime of life and thus deprived of the joy of a long and fruitful ministry for their Lord. But they were great in the courage they exhibited and in the sacrifice they made. Such a one was Kartar Singh, martyr for Christ in Tibet.

Details of Kartar's life, particularly of his adolescent years, are exceedingly difficult to find. His martyrdom was brought to the attention of the outside world by Sadhu Sundar Singh, who heard the account from an eyewitness during one of his missionary tours to Tibet. It is reasonably certain that Kartar was born in the last quarter of the nineteenth century and called upon to make the supreme sacrifice for his faith in the early years of our present century.

Kartar Singh, like Sadhu Sundar Singh, was a Sikh by

birth, the son of a rich landlord in the State of Patiala in India. All the hopes of the family were centered in this lad, for there were no other sons to carry on the name. He was brought up in the midst of luxury and given the best possible education in his youth. Nothing was forgotten that could make his training complete for the fulfillment of his father's ambitions for the boy.

But early in his youth there grew up in the mind of Kartar Singh a desire for spiritual things which his secular training could not satisfy. He heard of Christianity and little by little got to know and understand its claims, until an unshakable conviction of its truth laid hold of him. The more he studied about Christ, the more he felt that Christ alone could satisfy the longing of his soul, until at last he saw but one path: to follow the Savior for the rest of his life. He then took the irrevocable step of declaring himself a Christian, and it filled the hearts of his people with dismay.

When Kartar's father heard that he was about to become a Christian, he made every possible effort to prevent it. His father argued and implored, he commanded and threatened. He appealed to his son's family loyalty, he instigated communal pressures upon him. But Kartar's reply was, "Everywhere have I sought a Deliverer, but found him nowhere; now at last through his Word, God has revealed to me that the Savior is the Lord Jesus Christ, and now I shall not leave him who, in my stead, gave his life to save me."

Finally, Kartar's father sent to him the beautiful girl who was to be his wife. She told of her love for him, and pictured the happy life that they might have together. Kartar Singh was deeply touched by the girl's beauty and her declaration of love, but God gave him the grace to stand firm before this most severe temptation. With much tenderness he assured her of his love but insisted that, if he were forced to make a choice, his first loyalty was to Christ.

The brokenhearted girl returned to her would-be father-in-law and told him how useless had been her attempt. In a burst of anger the father called Kartar, disowned him as a son before the members of the family, and ordered him to remove all his clothes and leave the house immediately.

It was in the month of December and it was night. But Kartar had to obey. He took off his clothes, laid them at his father's feet and said, "Father, I am not ashamed today to divest myself of these clothes, because the righteousness of Jesus Christ has covered all my nakedness and sin." And then, naked and rejected, he left the house, praying as he went.

For two or three days Kartar Singh lived in the forest, tormented with hunger and cold. To secure enough money to buy food and a few clothes he took up the work of an ordinary "coolie" (laborer), and bent his back to tasks such as his own father's servants would have despised. To one reared in comfort this was indeed a humiliating and strenuous ordeal, but his heart was full of peace.

Very soon, however, Kartar adopted the yellow robe of a sadhu and began preaching among the towns and villages of Punjab State. When he was constrained by the love of Christ to preach in the regions beyond India, he turned his steps toward the land of Tibet, which for centuries had been closed to the gospel. On the way he took baptism at the hands of an Indian pastor and thus made the final break with the religion of his forefathers.

Before entering Tibet, Kartar remained in a border town for some months and with great determination gave himself to a concentrated study of the Tibetan language. Afterwards, preaching as he went, he made his way into the interior of that forbidden land.

Everywhere he went, Kartar Singh met with disdain and opposition. In one town the people seized him, bundled him up in a cloth, and, in turn bearing him upon their shoulders, took him outside their district and left him there. But no thought of going back to his homeland seems to have ever crossed his mind. These people were without Christ and were desperately in need of him; and as Christ had given his life, so Kartar was prepared to sacrifice his life also. He longed for the Tibetans to know of the love of the Heavenly Father.

In spite of numerous attempts to drive him out of Tibet, Kartar continued his preaching in many places for some time, but eventually he was hailed before the lama of Tsingham and charged with unlawfully entering the country and preaching a foreign religion.

The lama pronounced the death sentence upon him. Kartar heard his sentence without a quiver and with firm step walked with his accusers to the place of execution. On the way he delivered his last message, urging the crowd to seek salvation through Jesus Christ. As they ascended the hill, he said to them, "I shall not now descend from this place, but after three days I shall rise up to Heaven to be with my Lord."

At the place of execution Kartar was stripped of all his clothes and sewn up in a wet yak (Tibetan ox) skin and then exposed to the sun. As the sun shone, the hide gradually shrank and tightened about his body, causing his very bones to crack. A cruel, mocking crowd stood by to witness and laugh at his misery. On the ground at his side lay the New Testament that had been his one and only comfort through all his temptations and trials.

For three days this faithful servant of the Lord was subjected to this slow torture, but God's peace and joy kept flooding his soul. Over and over again he sang songs of praise and prayed for the salvation of his enemies. Finally on the third day, when Kartar knew that death was near, he requested that his right hand might be set free for a moment.

His plea was granted, probably more from curiosity than mercy. Collecting all his strength, Kartar wrote his last message on the fly-leaf of his Testament. Part of the message read thus:

I pray that my love for Him may not be less than that of the Hindu woman who burns along with the corpse of her dead husband. When for the dead husband, whom she may not hope to meet again, she does so much, how much more should I do for a living Lord who is moreover the Lord of life?

Then addressing the people, he said, "Are you standing by to see the death of a Christian? Come and gaze attentively, not that a Christian but death itself dies here. O Lord! Into Thy hands I commit my spirit because it is Thine." Shortly afterwards Kartar Singh died in the yak skin.

Among the crowd that witnessed the passing of this brave follower of the Cross was the chief secretary of the lama of Tsingham. He noticed the little New Testament in which Kartar had written his last message; he picked it up, carried it home, and started reading it.[1]

The witness and example of the courageous Christian from India had already prepared his heart for the message the Book had for him, and in reading it there came a new light and joy to him. As he pondered over God's Word he began to realize his sins and then to see the divine offer of forgiveness through Jesus Christ. After a few days he decided he should no longer keep his secret, so he stood before his master, the lama, and boldly declared his faith in Christ as Savior.

The lama was furious when he heard the witness of his secretary. He quickly called the court into session and

[1] The New Testament was written in the Urdu language of North India. It is not clear how the Tibetan secretary became familiar with this language, but it is quite possible that he had received his education in India.

pronounced upon him the death penalty. Like Kartar Singh, the chief secretary was sewn in a wet yak skin and put out into the sun to suffer a slow and cruel death. To add to his misery, his tormentors thrust red-hot skewers into his body. Then, as if they were weary of waiting for the inevitable end, they took him out of the yak skin, drove sharp bamboo splinters under the nails of his hands and feet, tied a rope around his mutilated body, and dragged him through the streets of the town. Finally they threw him on the dump heap outside the town and left him for dead.

For a long while he lay unconscious, but the cool night air slowly revived him. Little by little his strength returned, until he was able to crawl away to safety. When he had recovered from his many wounds he again appeared on the streets of the town, to the utter amazement of the entire populace. Superstitious fear of some supernatural power kept them from laying hands upon the Christian secretary, so that he was able to carry on a normal life in their midst and even testify publicly to the saving power of Jesus Christ.

This story of Kartar Singh and the secretary of Tsingham probably never would have become known to the outside world if it had not been for Sadhu Sundar Singh who happened to visit this town on one of his trips into Tibet. There he came in contact with the converted secretary who gave him the account in all its details.

But there is a postscript to this amazing story. Upon his return to India, Sadhu Sundar Singh found that Kartar Singh's father was still alive. He sought him out and told him the story of the death of his heroic son. As Sundar spoke of the great love of Christ exemplified in the death of Kartar, the old man listened with a softened heart. He finally said to the Christian sadhu, "I too believe in Him!"

14

The Sohn Family
of Korea

Pastor Sohn was a small, wiry man, full of energy, with a flash of fire in his eyes. Perpetually enthusiastic, whatever he did, he did with all his heart, "as unto the Lord."

During the Japanese occupation of Korea in 1910-45, when the authorities sought to impose the practice of emperor worship upon the Korean people, Sohn took a courageous stand against the order and even preached against it from his pulpit. After one such fiery denunciation, he was arrested by the Japanese, tried, and sentenced to serve a three-year term in prison. Though his confinement caused severe hardship to his family, Pastor Sohn refused to renounce his stand. His wife and children courageously bore the trial with him and carried on his work until his release from jail.

In 1945, at the close of World War II, the Reverend Sohn was serving as pastor to the inmates of the Leprosarium at Soon Chun, in Southwest Korea. The institution was full, so that Pastor Sohn often sought out the poorest and most needy of the leprous beggars roaming the streets of the city, sat with them, and divided his lunch among them. He won a good number of these social outcasts to faith in the Lord Jesus Christ and built a simple, inexpensive church building for them just outside the city limits.

When the United States Military Government took over after the war in Korea, they decided to train a "constabulary" for defense of the country. Training camps were organized in many centers. The underground Communist movement quickly took advantage of this plan and sent young men from the North, trained in subversive activity, to enlist in these camps.

One of these centers was located at Yusoo, a few miles distant from Soon Chun where Pastor Sohn lived and worked. His two sons were enrolled in the high school there.

By the spring of 1948, the Communists in the Yusoo training camp had completed their plans and were ready to strike. One morning in a surprise coup, they seized and shot the Korean officers, forcing the American advisers to flee for their lives. First the Communists took control of the army and then of the city. Shortly afterward they seized the town of Soon Chun. They spread the word around that Seoul, Taegu, Pusan, and other major cities had turned Communist and that soon all Korea would be liberated from capitalist tyranny.

The customary reign of terror began, while "kangaroo courts" were set up to try the "enemies of the people." The mob was duly roused by harangues and denunciations of all capitalists, landlords, and reactionaries. Then the defenseless "bourgeois" were dragged forward to be villified and condemned by the shouts of the mob. The Christians bore the brunt of this attack. Hundreds were lined up and shot; blood flowed like water.

Pastor Sohn's two sons in the high school at Yusoo had been publicly known as most active and ardent Christians, so it was inevitable that they would soon become marked by the Communists. About ten o'clock one morning, Communist students surrounded the house where the two boys lived, dragged them outside and began to beat the older one.

"For what crime are you beating me?" he cried out.

"You're an America lover. Aren't you planning to go to America to study?"

"I'm not an America lover. I am a servant of the Lord Jesus Christ."

"Ho, ho! A Christian!" they shouted in anger. "Religion is the opiate that the capitalists give to the common people to keep them in slavery. We're going to beat this superstition out of your foul body!"

"You can kill me but you cannot take the Lord Jesus out of my heart," came Tong In's reply.

Tong Sin, the younger of the two, began to try to defend his brother, but the gang then turned on him. Finally, both boys were dragged away to the Communist headquarters. The Red leaders tried to persuade the boys to renounce their faith and to join the party, but the Christian lads remained steadfast.

They were taken back of the government building and shown the scores of bodies of those who had been shot by order of the "People's Court."

Ahn Chae Sun, the leader, pointed with the end of his revolver to the pile of corpses. "Look at these," he said. "We give you one last chance. If you change your mind and come with us, you will live. If not, you will die."

"You can pull my insides out of my throat," was Tong In's reply, "but you cannot pull Jesus Christ out of my heart."

One of the students shouted, "What's the use in talking any longer. Kill him!"

The younger boy sprang in front of his brother. "Kill me, but spare my brother!"

Tong In pulled his brother back. "Why talk that way? They came to kill *me*. You go home and take care of our parents."

The Red students seized Tong In and blindfolded him.

"Why will you commit such a sin as this and go to hell?" he cried. "Believe in Jesus Christ and be saved!"

That infuriated Ahn Sun, the leader. He raised his revolver and fired. The Christian boy slumped to the ground.

Tong Sin rushed forward and embraced his brother's body. "He has gone to Heaven. I will follow him. Why did you shed the blood of an innocent boy? How are you going to get rid of this great sin? Repent and believe in the Lord Jesus Christ, and God will forgive you!"

One of the students shouted, "Kill that fellow too!"

Tong Sin cried, "Go ahead, then I can follow my brother to Heaven." He spread his arms in the shape of a cross. "I will also die in the likeness of a cross. Go ahead. Shoot me!"

A Red shouted, "This rascal is more evil than his brother. Kill him!"

Tong Sin closed his eyes and prayed aloud, "Father, forgive them, for they know not what they do. Bring them to repentance. Take care of my parents. Lord Jesus, receive my spirit."

The shot rang out.

When the news reached Pastor Sohn and his wife, they were smitten with grief. But God gave them grace to overcome the bitterness of their hearts.

Kind friends brought the bodies of the two young men to Soon Chun. Pastor Sohn said, "My two sons had intended to become ordained ministers to work among the lepers. Let them be buried in the leper burial ground."

The following day a great funeral service was held. All

the lepers were present and many Christians from the city.
Pastor Sohn himself led the service. Over the bowed heads of
the weeping congregation, his voice rang out clearly, "We
thank thee, Lord, that thou hast counted me worthy to be
the father of two martyrs. I thank thee for such precious
sons. . . . I thank thee, Lord, for giving me a heart full of
love toward those who killed them. Bring them to repentance
and save them. Grant unto me many spiritual children to
take the place of my sons."

Two days later, Government troops arrived and took
some of the mutinous Communists as prisoners. Ahn Chae Sun
was among this group. The others fled to the mountains.
Pastor Sohn heard this news. He sent his friend, Pastor Lah,
accompanied by Sohn's own daughter, to Yusoo, to ask the
soldiers to spare the life of Ahn Chae Sun, the one who had
shot the two boys.

When the Korean officer heard the request, he couldn't
believe his ears. "Are you crazy?" he asked Pastor Lah.
"No one would want to ask such a thing for the murderer
of his sons." But when he heard the request repeated from
the lips of the twelve-year-old girl standing at his side, he
decided he would investigate the matter for himself. With
Ahn Chae Sun, his prisoner, he drove to Soon Chun and sent
for Pastor Sohn.

"Is it true that you have asked that the life of the one who
killed your sons be spared?"

"Yes. My sons were ready to die. They were Christians.
This boy is not ready for he does not know the Lord Jesus.
Please put him in my keeping. Give him at least a stay of
execution. I shall send a request to President Syngman
Rhee, whom I know personally, for pardon. I want to tell
this boy of the Lord Jesus, so that he will be ready to die."

The colonel was stupefied. "I never heard of such love as
this," he declared. "It is beyond me. But I believe you are

sincere. I shall turn the young man over to you for your keeping, as you have asked. You must take full responsibility for him."

Pastor Sohn then asked Ahn Chae Sun where his parents lived. He took him to their home. They too could not understand why Pastor Sohn would spare their son. They received him with great courtesy and gratitude. Pastor Sohn remained in their home for a few days, telling them of the matchless love of God who sent his Son into the world to die for the sins of all mankind. Before he left for home, he had the inexplicable joy of leading the father, mother, and son into a personal relationship with Christ as Lord and Savior.

Then Ahn Chae Sun's parents requested Pastor Sohn to allow his daughter to come and live in their home. "We have no daughter of our own," they explained. "We want her to live with us and teach us day by day more about the Christian way. The love that you have shown us is beyond our human comprehension. We must receive this kind of love into our hearts."

Pastor Sohn knew that he and his wife would be lonely for their daughter if this strange request were granted. But after talking it over with the girl and praying about it, he decided to allow her to go for a time. He knew that with her loving and forgiving spirit she would teach them much about Christ's love.

The story of Pastor Sohn's magnanimity spread from person to person throughout southern Korea. It even reached the United States, so that a group of Christian young people composed a drama and presented the story to many audiences across the country. At the close of each performance an altar invitation was given, and many rededicated themselves to Christ, their Savior.

When the Korean War began in 1950, Communist armies pushed south and occupied the city of Soon Chun. Pastor

Sohn was urged by many friends to flee with other Christians, but he refused to leave his helpless leper friends. He continued to hold services in the church for them, and when he persisted in spite of an official ban by the Communists, he was arrested and thrown into prison.

When the prisoners, along with the Communists, heard the news of the Inchon landings by Allied forces, they expected soon to be set free. However, the Communists told them that they would be moved to another city at night. They took the prisoners out in small groups, and as each group was taken out, they were ambushed and shot. Pastor Sohn was among them. Their job done, the Communists fled. Only one man miraculously escaped death and was able to tell the story.

The next morning friends recovered the body of Pastor Sohn and buried him in the leper cemetery beside his two sons.

There is a final note of triumph in the story. Ahn Chae Sun, the Communist student who had murdered the two boys, became a Christian and dedicated his life to take the place of those whom he had slain. He entered the Koryu Theological Seminary in Pusan. At a memorial service for Pastor Sohn, he said, "I stand here as a modern Saul of Tarsus. I was once a persecutor of the Christians, but now I am a preacher of the Gospel!"

Bibliography

Chapter I Ko Tha Byu

Anderson, Courtney. *To the Golden Shore, The Life of Adoniram Judson.* Boston: Little and Brown, 1956.

Marshall, Harry Ignatius. *Flashes Along the Burma Road.* New York: Island Press, 1946.

Mason, Francis. *A Memoir of Ko Tha Byu.* Insein, Burma: Burman Theological Seminary, 1938.

Montgomery, Helen. *Following the Sunrise.* Philadelphia: American Baptist Publication Society, 1913.

Wylie, Mrs. Macleod. *The Gospel in Burmah.* London: W. H. Dalton, 1895.

Chapter II Chi-oang and Do-wai

Brand, Edward. *He Brought Them Out.* London: British and Foreign Bible Society, 1949.

Cheng, Lien-min. *A Short History of the Presbyterian Church Among the Mountain Tribes in Taiwan.* New York: Occasional Bulletin from the Missionary Research Library, April–May, 1965.

Copeland, Margaret L. *Chi-Oang, Mother of the Taiwan Tribes Church.* Taipei, Taiwan: United Publishing Centre, 1962.

Dickson, James. *Stranger than Fiction.* Toronto: Evangelical Publishers, 1948.

Dickson, Lillian. *These My People; Serving Christ Among the Mountain People of Formosa.* Grand Rapids, Michigan: Zondervan Publishing House, 1958.

Tong, Hollington K. *Christianity in Taiwan: A History.* Taipei: China Post, 1961.

Chapter III   Bishop Crowther

Burton, Margaret E. *Comrades in Service.* New York: Y.W.C.A., 1915.

Creegan, C. C. *Great Missionaries.* New York: Thomas Y. Crowell & Company, 1895.

Neill, Stephen. *A History of Christian Missions.* Grand Rapids, Michigan: William B. Eerdmans Publishing Co., 1965.

Page, Jesse. *The Black Bishop.* London: Simpkins, Marshall, Hamilton, Kent and Co., 1910.

Stock, Eugene. *History of the Church Missionary Society,* Volume II. London: Church Missionary Society, 1899.

Webster, James Bertin. *The African Churches Among the Yoruba.* Oxford: Clarendon Press, 1964.

Chapter IV   Bishop Azariah

Azariah, V. S. *Christian Giving.* New York: Association Press, 1955.

Eddy, Sherwood. *Pathfinders of the World Missionary Crusade.* Nashville: Abingdon Press, 1945.

Mathews, Basil. *Forward Through the Ages.* New York: Friendship Press, 1960.

Smith, Eugene L. *God's Mission—and Ours.* Nashville: Abingdon Press, 1961.

Whitehead, Henry. Article entitled "Vedanayagam Samuel Azariah," in *International Review of Missions,* April, 1945.

Chapter V   Tamil David

Life of Tamil David. Madras, India: The Madras Bible Warehouse, 1950.

Chapter VI   John Sung

Ling—Liu Yih. *Life of John Sung* (in Chinese). Kowloon, Hong Kong: Christian Witness Press, 1962.

Leo, Micah W. M. and Wang, Thomas T. H. *Voice in the Wilderness* (in Chinese). Detroit, Michigan: Chinese Christian Mission, 1961.

Lyall, Leslie T. *Flame for God in the Far East.* Chicago: Moody Press, 1954.

Chapter VII Pandita Ramabai

Butler, Clementina. *Pandita Ramabai.* Westwood, N.J.: Fleming H. Revell, 1922.

Fuller, Mary Lucie Bierce. *Triumph of an Indian Widow.* New York: Christian Alliance Publishing Co., 1928.

Mathews, Basil. *Pandita Ramabai: India's Christian Pilgrim.* Grand Rapids, Michigan: Zondervan Publishing House, 1949.

Chapter VIII Joseph Hardy Neesima

Davis, Jerome D. *Joseph Hardy Neesima.* Westwood, N.J.: Fleming H. Revell, 1894.

—————. *Effective Workers in Needy Fields.* New York: Student Volunteer Movement, 1902.

Hardy, Arthur Sherburne. *Life and Letters of Joseph Hardy Neesima.* Boston: Houghton, Mifflin and Co., 1892.

Latourette, Kenneth Scott. *These Sought a Country.* New York: Harper and Brothers, 1950.

Pritchard, Marianna and Norman. *Ten Against the Storm.* New York: Friendship Press, 1957.

Chapter IX Chief Khama

Brain, Belle M. *From Every Tribe and Nation.* Westwood, N.J.: Fleming H. Revell, 1927.

Gollock, G. A. *Sons of Africa.* New York: Friendship Press, 1928.

Harris, J. C. *Khama, the Great African Chief.* (Publisher Unknown.)

Lovett, Richard. *The History of the London Missionary Society.* Volume I. Henry Frowde, 1899.

Mathews, Basil. *The Book of Missionary Heroes.* New York: George H. Doran Company, 1922.

Chapter X Toyohiko Kagawa

Axling, William. *Kagawa.* New York: Harper and Brothers, 1946.

Baumann, Margaret. *Kagawa, an Apostle of Japan.* New York: The Macmillan Company, 1936.

Davey, Cyril J. *Kagawa of Japan.* Nashville: Abingdon Press, 1961.

Saunders, Kenneth. *Whither Asia? A Study of Three Leaders.* New York: The Macmillan Company, 1933.

Van Baalen, Jan Karel. *Kagawa, the Christian.* Grand Rapids, Michigan: William B. Eerdmans Publishing Co., 1936.

Chapter XI William Wade Harris

Gollock, G. A. *Sons of Africa.* New York: Friendship Press, 1928.

Platt, J. W. *An African Prophet.* London: S.C.M. Press.

Chapter XII   Sadhu Sundar Singh

Sundar Singh. *The Cross Is Heaven*. Ed. by A. J. Appasamy. New York: Association Press, 1957.

Davey, Cyril J. *The Yellow Robe, The Story of Sadhu Sundar Singh*. London: S.C.M. Press, 1950.

Heiler, Friedrich. *The Gospel of Sadhu Sundar Singh*. London: George Allen and Unwin, 1927.

Parker, Mrs. Arthur. *Sadhu Sundar Singh: Called of God*. Westwood, N.J.: Fleming H. Revell Co., 1920.

Streeter, B. H. and Appasamy, A. J. *The Sadhu*. London: Macmillan and Co., 1927.

Chapter XIII   Kartar Singh

Parker, Mrs. Arthur. *Sadhu Sundar Singh: Called of God*. Westwood, N.J.: Fleming H. Revell Co., 1920.

Chapter XIV   The Sohn Family of Korea

Campbell, Arch. *The Christ of the Korean Heart*. Secunderabad, India: Good News Literature Center, 1954.

Index

219

3